Canoeing and Kayaking Ohio's Streams

Canoeing and Kayaking Ohio's Streams

An Access Guide
for Paddlers and Anglers

Rick Combs and Steve Gillen

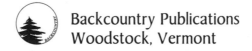

Backcountry Publications
Woodstock, Vermont

Invitation to the reader

Rivers and streams are particularly given to altering their courses, and with time, bridges, roads, access points, and landmarks also change. If you find that changes have occurred on the waterways described in this book, please let the author and publisher know, so that corrections can be made in future editions. Other comments and suggestions for additional river trips are also welcome. Address all correspondence to:

> Editor, Canoeing
> Backcountry Publications
> P.O. Box 175
> Woodstock, VT 05091-0175

Canoeing and Kayaking Ohio's Streams was originally published in 1983 in two volumes by The Menasha Ridge Press, under the title *A Canoeing and Kayaking Guide to the Streams of Ohio*, Volumes I and II (ISBN 0-89732-012-3 and 0-89732-013-1). All material retained from the original edition has been thoroughly checked and updated.

Published by Backcountry Publications,
A Division of The Countryman Press, Inc.
Woodstock, Vermont 05091-0175

Library of Congress Cataloging-in-Publication Data
Combs, Rick, 1952–
Canoeing and kayaking Ohio's streams : an access guide for paddlers and anglers / Rick Combs and Steve Gillen.
    p.   cm.
Based on: A canoeing and kayaking guide to the streams of Ohio, © 1983.
ISBN 0-88150-252-9
1. Canoes and canoeing—Ohio—Guidebooks.   2. Kayaking—Ohio—Guidebooks.   3. Fishing—Ohio—Guidebooks.   4. Rivers—Ohio—Recreational use—Guidebooks.   5. Ohio—Guidebooks.   I. Gillen, Steve, 1953–.   II. Gillen, Steve, 1953–   Canoeing and kayaking guide to the streams of Ohio.   III. Title.
GV776.03C65   1994
797.1'22'09771—dc20   93-45778
                                                               CIP

Cover photograph by David Brownell
Interior photographs by the authors, unless otherwise indicated
Maps by Paul Woodward, Mapline Cartographic Services
Cover design by Georganna Towne
Text design and page composition by Carlson Design Studio
Printed in the United States of America
10 9 8 7 6 5 4 3 2 1

Dedication

*For Sarah, David, Hillary, and generations of paddlers to come,
who will find Ohio's streams the way we leave them*

Ohio's Streams

Streams of the Northwest

Streams of the Northeast

Michigan

Lake Erie

WILLIAMS

Tiffin R.

St. Joseph R.

FULTON

LUCAS

Toledo

OTTAWA

Toussaint C.

Maumee R.

DEFIANCE

WOOD

SANDUSKY

ERIE

LORAIN

Vermilion R.

Black R.

Rocky R.

LAKE

Chagrin R.

ASHTABULA

Cleveland

CUYAHOGA

GEAUGA

Grand R.

Ashtabula R.

Conneaut C.

Conneaut C.

Ohio

Pennsylvania

HENRY

portage R.

SENECA

HURON

MEDINA

SUMMIT

PORTAGE

TRUMBULL

PAULDING

PUTNAM

HANCOCK

Blanchard R.

Aglaize R.

Tinkers C.

Cuyahoga R.

Akron

MAHONING

VAN WERT

Sandusky R.

ALLEN

WYANDOT

CRAWFORD

ASH-
LAND

WAYNE

Mohican R.

Walhonding R.

Tuscarawas R.

Killbuck C.

STARK

COLUMBIANA

L. Beaver C.

St. Marys R.

RICH-
LAND

Indiana

MERCER

AUGLAIZE

HARDIN

Scioto R.

Olentangy R.

MARION

MORROW

HOLMES

TUS-
CARAWAS

CARROLL

JEFFER-
SON

SHELBY

LOGAN

KNOX

COSHOCTON

HARRISON

Greenville C.

Stillwater R.

MIAMI

CHAMPAIGN

UNION

DELAWARE

Kokosing R.

LICKING

Licking R.

MUSKINGUM

GUERNSEY

BELMONT

DARKE

Mad R.

FRANKLIN

Columbus

Muskingum R.

PREBLE

Fourmile C.

CLARK

MADISON

Big Darby C.

FAIRFIELD

NOBLE

MONROE

L. Muskingum R.

Dayton

MONT-
GOMERY

GREENE

PICKAWAY

PERRY

MORGAN

WASHINGTON

BUTLER

Great Miami R.

WAR-
REN

Little Miami R.

CLINTON

FAYETTE

Paint C.

ROSS

Scioto R.

HOCKING

Hocking R.

Rush

ATHENS

**Streams
of the East**

HAMILTON

Stonelick C.

CLINTON

HIGHLAND

Rocky Fork C.

Paint C.

Cincinnati

CLER-
MONT

White Oak C.

Ohio Brush C.

PIKE

VINTON

Raccoon C.

MEIGS

West
Virginia

Ohio

BROWN

ADAMS

SCIOTO

JACKSON

GALLIA

River

LAWRENCE

**Streams of
the Southwest**

Kentucky

The Muskingum System

The Scioto System

**Streams of
South Central Ohio**

50 statute miles

N

MapLine / Paul Woodward — © 1994 The Countryman Press, Inc.

Table of Contents

Preface and Acknowledgments

In this second edition of our guide we have endeavored to improve upon both the content and format of our earlier effort. We have consolidated what had been two volumes, avoiding much duplication and producing a more conveniently sized book. Throw it in a pack or tackle box. Take it on the stream. Use it. Abuse it. We'll make more.

Mark it up with your notes and comments. Access hard to find? Give us a better description. Is there a prominent feature we've neglected to mention? Let us know. Have we overlooked your favorite fish? Set us straight. Drop a photocopy of your notes in the mail to The Countryman Press, P.O. Box 175, Woodstock, Vermont 05091-0175, and they'll forward it to us. If we use your idea in the next edition, we'll send you a new book, autographed, with our thanks, no charge, and we'll acknowledge your help in the next edition. For now, our thanks to all those who called or wrote to offer suggestions, improvements, and additional information on the first edition; and thanks to all those who provided encouragement for this revision.

For paddlers, we have added coverage of Stonelick Creek, a tiny but occasionally intimidating stretch of expert-only white water. To help you get oriented, we have dramatically improved the quality and readability of the maps and have provided more detailed descriptions of access points.

For anglers, in addition to access directions, we have provided information about typical fish species—bass, catfish, panfish, and so on. But our focus has been on game fish of special interest: salmon, steelhead, trout, walleye, pike, muskie, and seasonal smallmouth runs.

Friends always help in the production of a book. While space limitations prevent us from acknowledging all the cooperative people who contributed to our efforts, we'd like to thank those who were especially enthusiastic in sharing their time and expertise to help make this book possible:

Bob Sehlinger of Menasha Ridge Press
Jim Carpenter of the Miami Group Sierra Club
Dick Teeple of the Toledo River Gang
Mike Sullivan of Ohio River Forecasters
Tip Carpenter of the Columbus AYH
Jim Hopewell of the ODNR
John Kopec of the ODNR
Tom and Mary Jo Suhar of the Miami Group Sierra Club
Harry Barefoot of Barefoot Canoes
George Palmiter (whose tireless efforts to preserve and beautify Ohio's streams have won national acclaim and served as models for other states)
Chuck Tummonds of the ACA
Dick Parsons

This book wouldn't have been possible without the generous assistance of the folks we have named and countless other paddlers across the state, paddlers who were sometimes understandably reluctant to surrender information about their favorite streams for publication. If you do search out sections of the streams we have described, please keep that fact in mind and do not betray our friend's trust in us as responsible authors or their trust in you as responsible paddlers. Be courteous to those you encounter, both on the water and on the adjacent banks. Be respectful of the interests of property owners and other paddlers. Leave no trace of your passage other than the swirl behind your paddle. And if you're able, take with you some of the remnants left by others not so thoughtful. Only by doing so ourselves can we all enjoy the paddling that Ohio's waterways afford.

Note: "ODNR" stands for "Ohio Department of Natural Resources." Access points marked "ODNR" are maintained by the Department, and photos credited "ODNR" were provided by the Department.

Getting the Lay of the Land: Water, Weather, and Ice

Water: The Hydrologic Cycle

The most basic concept about water is the hydrologic or water cycle, which moves water from the earth to the atmosphere and back again. Several things happen to water that falls to the earth: it becomes surface runoff draining directly into rivers or their tributaries, it is retained by the soil and used by plants, it may be returned directly to the atmosphere through evaporation, or it becomes groundwater by filtering down through subsoil and layers of rock.

To say that all paddlers must have a thorough knowledge of the hydrologic cycle, stream morphology, geology, and fluid dynamics is undoubtedly overstating the case. An intuitive grasp of the forces at work in moving water is more than sufficient for the majority of paddlers in the majority of paddling situations. Nevertheless, a broad exposure to the basic concepts and processes involved when water moves from high to low elevations and back again enhances a paddler's awareness and appreciation of the natural forces that can make the sport at times soothing, at times exhilarating, and at times life-threatening.

A threshold question for paddlers considering a trip down any Ohio stream on any given day is: can it float a boat? Or from the angler's perspective, is the water low enough to be fishable? We've attempted to help you address these questions by supplying phone numbers for information about stream conditions for each stream in this guide, but paddler's instinct and some background information will help you draw correct preliminary conclusions.

Variations in the flow levels of watercourses are based in large part on fluctuations in rainfall. Complicating the picture is the influence of local soil conditions, plant life, terrain slope, ground cover, and air temperature. In summer, during the peak growing season, water is used more readily by plants, and high air temperatures encourage increased evaporation. The fall and winter low-water periods are caused by decreased precipitation; however, the frozen ground and the limited use of water by plants means that abnormally high amounts of rain during these seasons, or water from melting snow, can cause flash floods because surface runoff is high—there's no place for the water to go but into creeks and rivers.

Ohio Weather

Ohio's climate can be described as moderate. As a result of the relatively small range in latitude, the compact shape of the state, and the absence of mountain ranges, the climate is more or less uniform across the state. Minor regional deviations from this pattern are the results of Lake Erie to the north and the rugged topography of the unglaciated plateau to the southeast.

Temperature

Average annual temperatures in Ohio are moderate, varying less than 10°F from north to south. Because Ohio has pronounced seasonal shifts in temperature, however, the temperature extremes are most valuable in evaluating climate and weather patterns. The annual temperature range is about 45°F (the difference between the mean temperatures of the hottest and coldest months). The range in daily temperatures varies from 20° to 24°F in summer and from 16°

to 20°F in winter. This range in daily temperatures differs from north to south, with the daily ranges somewhat lower in the north because of the moderating effect of the Great Lakes on air temperatures. In an average year, 90-degree heat may be expected about 20 times in summer. Readings of 0°F or lower can be expected on fewer than four days each winter.

High temperatures are not usually a problem for paddlers, and indeed they may be desirable. Very low temperatures and frozen streams may make paddling impossible. In between the extremes of temperature are chilly days (or moderate days and chilly water) that can present a danger of hypothermia (see page 15).

Precipitation

Averaging 37 inches per year, precipitation in Ohio is slightly above the national average. Over the state's more than 41,000 square miles, 37 inches of rain, snow, sleet, and hail amounts to 27 *trillion* gallons of water. Two-thirds of this water, or 18 trillion gallons, is either evaporated or transpired by plants, leaving 9 trillion gallons as groundwater and runoff to support the state's waterways. The amount of annual rainfall can, however, vary widely from year to year, and recorded Ohio averages have ranged from a low of 26 inches to a high of over 50 inches.

Ohio's precipitation is seasonally well-distributed, with slight peaks in early spring and again in midsummer when thunderstorm activity increases. April is the wettest month, with an average of 4 inches of precipitation; October, on the other hand, is the driest month, with an average of 2.5 inches of precipitation. This seasonal distribution varies geographically across the state, as does the annual precipitation average and the form in which it occurs.

The northern part of the state tends to receive relatively more precipitation in early spring, while the central and southern parts of the state tend to receive more precipitation in midsummer—the results of seasonally changing storm paths and different geographical features that create the primary exception to Ohio's otherwise uniform climate and weather patterns. In winter months there is a great deal more storm activity in the northeastern counties. Winds from the north must cross Lake Huron and the widest part of Lake Erie, picking up moisture and heat from these large bodies of water. The warm, moist air is lifted quickly as it is forced southward over the divide between the St. Lawrence and Ohio River drainage systems. Cooling as it rises, the air releases its moisture in the form of snow, giving this region a reputation as the state's snowbelt. This weather pattern may produce in excess of 100 inches of snowfall in any given year in the northeastern counties. (Note, however, that this figure does not mean 100 inches of precipitation, as it may take as much as 10 inches of snow to make 1 inch of water.) In contrast, the same year may see less than 16 inches of snow to the south along the Ohio River.

At other times of the year the central and southern parts of the state receive more precipitation, which results from the combined effects of warm-weather, rain-producing storm paths across these sections of the state and the presence of rough, unglaciated terrain that causes air masses to rise and fall, cooling as they rise and giving up their moisture in the process.

On the average there are 120 days of measurable precipitation in Ohio each year. A typical year consists of 134 clear days, 107 partly cloudy days, and 124 cloudy days.

Long summer dry spells will reduce most of the streams discussed in this guidebook to barely passable waterways. On the other hand, storms dropping an inch or more of rain in any 24-hour period will often put those same streams at near-flood conditions. For most of us, a happy medium lies somewhere between the stream-bottom rocks and the bankside trees—you want to stay out of both.

Ohio Topography: Ice Age Sculpture

Ohio's paddlers are confronted with a state that has neither extremes of elevations, extremes of latitude, nor extremes of climate. The natural presumption is that all of Ohio's rivers must look alike. But despite the fact that Ohio lacks spectacular mountains, deep canyons, rain forests, and deserts, the topography and vegetation within its boundaries vary widely. An understanding of why this is so, and an appreciation of the practical consequences of the state's topography, require a brief examination of the four major events in Ohio's geologic history.

During the Paleozoic era, 200–400 million years ago, Ohio was covered by an ocean. Over the eons, particulates settled to the bottom of this ocean, leaving layers of various kinds of rock: limestone, dolomites, shale, sandstone, and conglomerates.

Dramatic scenery, rock arches—the Ohio that can't be seen from the interstate is available to paddlers who seek it.

After many years the ocean receded, leaving parts of Ohio covered by swamps. The lush vegetation grew and died, falling into the water and piling into thick layers of partly rotted plants. After much compression, these thick layers eventually became deposits of bituminous coal.

Forces deep in the earth then caused an upheaval in the crust that tilted these layers on an eastward-sloping angle, creating a series of steps from west to east. Each step was composed of one of the layers of underlying rock. The exposed layers in the northwestern half of the state became part of a region designated the Central Highlands. The exposed layers in the southeastern half of the state became part of the Appalachian Plateau.

Finally, during the Pleistocene epoch, 1 million to 10,000 years ago (commonly referred to as the Ice Age), glaciers pushed down from Canada, clipped off the tops of these steps, and filled in the valleys with glacial till (clay, mud, sand, gravel, and boulders). The glaciers left their unmistakable impression on most of the state (only 33 counties in the southeastern corner of the state are unglaciated), and the vast majority of Ohio's streams and natural lakes, including Lake Erie, date from this epoch.

These major geologic events left Ohio divided into five distinct landform regions: 1) the Unglaciated Appalachian Plateau; 2) the

Glaciated Appalachian Plateau; 3) the Central Lowland, covered largely by glacial deposits and called the Till Plains; 4) the Lake Plains, composed of a succession of beds left by the receding ancestors of Lake Erie; and 5) the very limited portion of the Central Lowland, which was never glaciated and is usually referred to as the Lexington Plain. (See Figure 1.)

Unglaciated Appalachian Plateau

The Unglaciated Appalachian Plateau, a mature hill country lying in the southeastern quarter of the state, began as a plateau of moderate elevation deeply dissected by streams tributary to the Ohio River. It now consists of narrow ridges and rounded hillocks separated by steep-sided valleys up to 300 feet in depth. Primarily as a result of the rugged topography, this region is still sparsely settled (relatively speaking), and over half the total surface area is covered by some type of forest. Originally this forest was composed mainly of white oak, black oak, and shagbark hickory. Now, however, much of it is second growth of inferior composition.

Glaciated Appalachian Plateau

The western and northern edges of the Appalachian Plateau have been modified by glaciation. Glacial erosion has rounded and smoothed the hills, and glacial deposition has broadened and flattened the valleys. These changes have altered the original drainage, resulting in the addition of small lakes and poorly drained depressions.

Because the topography is less rugged in this region than it is in the unglaciated plateau, the natural forest cover has surrendered to more extensive settlement. What remains is primarily a mixture of oak, hickory, beech, and maple, with no particular species predominating.

Till Plains

The Till Plains cover over one-third of Ohio and constitute the part of the state most obviously affected by glaciation. The bedrock is covered by loose materials deposited by the glaciers (in many places to depths of more than 100 feet). The surface is generally level, although there are low ridges (called moraines) that formed wherever the edge of the ice paused in its erratic retreat. The presence of

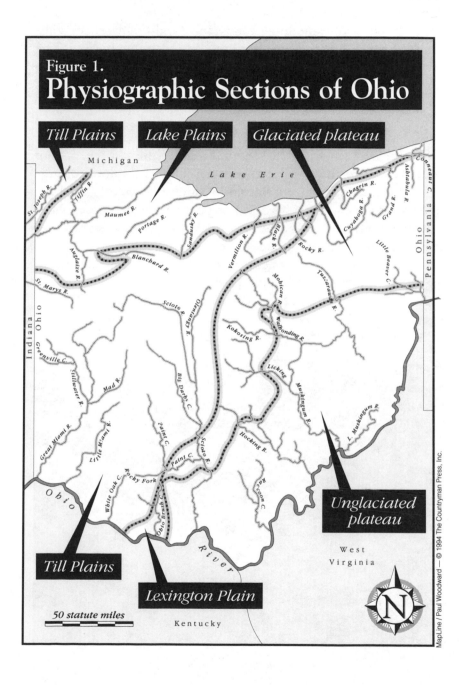

Figure 1.
Physiographic Sections of Ohio

Till Plains

Lake Plains

Glaciated plateau

Unglaciated plateau

Till Plains

Lexington Plain

50 statute miles

occasional moraines notwithstanding, relief over large areas of the Till Plains is less than 100 feet.

Because of the smoothed topography and the excellent soils, much of the Till Plains area has been settled and cultivated. The settlement pattern is more related to roads and access than it is to topography and streams. The natural vegetation that remains includes beech forests, prairie grasses, and freshwater swamps.

Lake Plains

By far the flattest part of the state, the Lake Plains region does not exhibit characteristics of glaciation so much as it exhibits characteristics of sedimentation from the diminishing ancestors of Lake Erie. There are no moraines here; the most prominent topographical feature is a series of sandy beach ridges, each only a few feet high and each marking the edge of one of the earlier lakes.

While this area was once covered by a nearly impenetrable swamp forest—the Black Swamp—by 1885 it had been drained, cleared, and settled. Now the road pattern is rectangular, the average distance between houses in the rural areas is slightly more than 0.1 mile, and a village or city pops up every 6 to 10 miles.

Paddling Ohio's streams offers an unspoiled view of the state not all that different from what the first trappers and explorers might have seen. [ODNR photo]

Lexington Plain

The Lexington Plain is the smallest physiographic region in the state; it is also the most unique. The unusual topography is the result of stream erosion of limestone bedrock. The terrain is characterized by broad, flat-topped ridges irregularly dissected by steep ravines, hollows, and sink holes. Settlement in this region has been concentrated on the flat ridge tops, leaving the steep slopes bordering the streams covered with mixed forests.

2

Paddler Information

Safety

It doesn't take a computer analysis to reveal a pattern in Ohio boating accidents: the majority of fatalities on Ohio's streams are caused by rivers at or near flood stage, low-head dams, and/or an absence of life preservers. In Ohio very few canoeing and kayaking fatalities involve experienced paddlers, because they always wear personal flotation devices (PFDs) and they stay away from dams.

PFDs

Coast Guard–approved PFDs should be worn at all times on the water. Type I and II vests are designed to help keep the wearer's face out of the water even if he or she is unconscious. Type III PFDs include ski vests and life preservers designed specifically for canoeing, kayaking, and other water sports. They are more comfortable than Type I and II vests but will not ordinarily keep an unconscious person's face out of the water.

Parents should set a good example by wearing life jackets.

Low-head Dams and Hydraulics

According to an Ohio Division of Watercraft publication concerning river rescue techniques, "If an engineer set out to design an efficient, unattended, self-operating drowning machine, it would be hard to come up with anything more effective than a low-head dam." Unfortunately, these small flood-control dams are among the most common hazards on midwestern streams.

There were hundreds of low-head dams in Ohio by the 1960s. Some of these old dams are maintained, others are in the process of washing out, and occasionally a new one is still built. Although we have marked numerous low-head dams on the stream maps in this guidebook, we cannot guarantee that every low-head dam in the state is indicated on these maps or stream tables. Paddlers must exercise caution and be alert to the presence of dams on all Ohio streams. A low rumble and a smooth horizon line at the downstream end of a river pool are warning signs that you are approaching a dam or waterfall. Ferry to shore and approach with caution.

Fatalities involving low-head dams typically occur on rivers at or near flood stage and generally involve untrained paddlers who lack sufficient control of their craft to back-paddle, ferry, or in some way maneuver their boats to shore in moderate to swift currents. They are swept over a dam despite frantic attempts to avoid it. Also at high risk are inexperienced paddlers who, seeing that at high water levels a dam is nearly submerged, are deceived into believing they can run it.

The most dangerous factor associated with low-head dams is the hydraulic (or backwash) below them (see photograph of low-head dam on page 78). A hydraulic occurs any time water passes over an obstruction. Surface water downstream from the obstruction actually flows upstream to fill in the depression created by the force of the falling water. Anything falling over the obstacle will, if the hydraulic is a strong one, be washed under the water to surface a short distance downstream, only to be carried back to the obstruction by the backwash and submerged to repeat the cycle. Even small hydraulics can be dangerous. Paddlers are sometimes eventually washed out of moderately strong hydraulics. A paddler who becomes caught in a powerful hydraulic—the kind frequently formed by low-head dams— will most likely not survive it.

Paddlers sometimes refer to "keeper" hydraulics. A hydraulic exists below every obstacle in a river, but most natural obstacles create hydraulics that are strong in the center and weak at the left and right edges. A keeper is a hydraulic that is uniform in strength from side to side, making it difficult for a swimmer to find an opening. These keepers are most frequently found below low-head dams or ledge-type falls. They "keep" you from swimming out.

Flooded Streams

Most low-head dam fatalities occur on the swollen rivers of early spring. Apart from the dams, however, flooded rivers offer a host of dangers for paddlers. They're likely to be full of floating debris such as washed-down trees and other obstacles.

The faster current of a river in spring allows less reaction time and makes back-paddling and ferrying around obstacles more diffi-cult. The river is also wider and deeper at flood stage, making for long swims in the event of a capsize. Perhaps most important, when the paddler decides it's time to get off the river, he or she is likely to discover that in spring conditions there are no banks to get out on. Rock gardens and strong current differentials are one thing; navigat-ing at high speed through second-growth timber and brier patches is too much even for the experts.

Summer thunderstorms can make any Ohio stream treacherous. As one recent, albeit extreme, example, a storm in June of 1990 dropped five inches of rain in a three-hour period on the Wegee Creek drainage basin near Shadyside, Ohio. At peak, the torrent's 55,000 cubic feet of water per second moved down this ordinarily tranquil valley, sweeping away homes and killing 26 people. That's more than twice the volume of water ordinarily carried by the mighty Ohio River. You wouldn't have been tempted to paddle Wegee Creek that day, and while you might be tempted to paddle other streams at less extreme levels, you should stay off any stream when the water has risen into the bankside trees.

Strainers and Logjams

Strainers and logjams are common hazards on midwestern streams. Strainers are usually trees that have fallen into or across streams but, strictly speaking, are anything that water flows through but boats and paddlers don't. They are commonly encountered on the outer edges of turns, where erosion has undercut trees, eventually causing them to fall into the stream. The outer edge of a turn is also where

At higher water levels, this deadfall would probably present a risk of entrapment. [ODNR photo]

the current is swiftest. (This is why blind turns should be navigated along the inside banks whenever possible. Strainers occur far less frequently there, and the slower current affords more time to react to any contingency.)

When hitting a strainer (or any other obstacle) is inevitable, lean the boat downstream, taking care to avoid getting caught between the boat and the obstruction. The tendency is for the current to flip the boat upstream. The gunwale dips quickly below the surface, the boat fills instantly with water, and it is swept under or pinned against the strainer. In a current of only five miles per hour, a 16-foot canoe full of water will be pushed downstream with a force of 2,240 pounds; downstream from a swamped canoe is not the place to be. Remember: because of strainers, even the slowest, most pastoral stream of the type so common in Ohio can be dangerous.

If you come out of your boat, stay with it if possible—but get to the upstream end immediately. If you are thrown clear of your boat, or if it appears safer to abandon it, float on your back with your feet pointed downstream, your toes out of the water—your feet and legs make better shock absorbers than your head. If you strike out for shore, don't try to compensate for the current and waste energy swimming upstream or time swimming downstream, but head directly for shore. Finally, don't try to stand up until you're in slow, shallow water.

Hypothermia

Hypothermia poses a serious threat to fall, winter, and spring paddlers in Ohio. Hypothermia involves a loss of body heat so sudden or prolonged that the body is unable to generate sufficient warmth to replace it. Individuals vary in sensitivity to cold and the likelihood of suffering from hypothermia. Rate of metabolism, body fat, even fear can all be important factors. Symptoms include violent shivering, loss of coordination, muscle spasms, confusion, and drunken behavior. In severe cases victims become unconscious and may become blue-gray in color.

A spill into water that is only slightly above 32°F can result in hypothermia in a matter of minutes, but even 50°F water is unbearably cold. Mild spring days have become nightmares for paddlers who weren't prepared for frigid water. A combination of cold water, a light breeze, and inadequate clothing can be deadly. (You needn't take a spill to be in danger of hypothermia; paddlers subject to spray and waves splashing into the boat can also get into serious trouble.)

There are several ways to prevent hypothermia. First, proper clothing is essential. The most effective clothing is a good wet suit.

Cold-weather gear should include a wet suit to prevent hypothermia. [ODNR photo]

A simple formula to keep in mind is that if the combined air and water temperature is less than 100°F, wet suits are in order. At combined temperatures of 100°–125°F, wet suits are recommended, especially for inexperienced paddlers. If you don't own a wet suit and plan to paddle in cold water, you might consider renting a suit from a dive shop. Dive suits can be rented inexpensively and are quite effective, although not as comfortable as wet suits made specifically for canoeists and kayakers.

A common alternative, when water is on the cold side but air temperatures are warm, is to wear wool. Wool retains much of its insulating properties when wet. Light cotton and some synthetics have the advantage of drying quickly. Denim jeans make poor boating apparel. (A disproportionate number of hypothermia victims have worn jeans. They may be popular, but they soak up water like a wick and take forever to dry.) Nylon windbreakers can be effective in reducing wind chill; they also help hold in body heat. It's a good idea to take a change of clothes, some paper, and matches (a butane lighter is even better) in a dry bag whenever you paddle on cold water.

Hypothermia victims must have heat from an external source. Get them out of wet clothes and into dry ones if possible. Skin-to-skin contact is highly effective; if you can, get the victim into a sleeping bag with another person. Never let a hypothermia victim go to sleep; build a fire and feed the victim hot liquids.

If a house is nearby, as is often the case on Ohio streams, get the hypothermia victim inside by all means. Hot baths are fine in mild cases, but in severe cases, particularly when the victim is unconscious, hot baths are extremely dangerous because they can speed up circulation too quickly, returning cold blood from the extremities to the trunk, resulting in still lower body temperatures or even cardiac arrest. Even in milder cases, where the hot-bath treatment is opted for, it is safer to lower only the victim's trunk into the water, holding the extremities out.

External cardiac massage or mouth-to-mouth resuscitation may be necessary in extreme cases of hypothermia. Remember that slowed metabolic rates can make revival possible long after a pulse or breathing has become indiscernible. As with drowning victims, slowed metabolic rates caused by extremely cold water have made possible seemingly miraculous resuscitations, even in cases where victims were submerged for long periods. There are well-documented cases of people submerged in frigid water for 40 minutes and longer who were revived by cardiac massage or mouth-to-mouth resuscitation.

Instruction

Perhaps the most important factor to stress in any discussion of water safety is the value of training. Exercising common sense can go a long way toward ensuring your safety on the river, but there is no substitute for proper instruction. A training program will not only make your paddling excursions safer, it will immeasurably enhance your enjoyment of the sport. There are many canoe and kayak organizations in Ohio, and most of them offer excellent weekend training sessions (see Appendix C). Find a group in your area and get involved—you'll learn a lot, have a great time, and meet people who share your enthusiasm for canoeing or kayaking and the outdoors.

Rating the River

For many years concerned paddlers have attempted to rate rivers objectively. Central among their tools for doing so has been the International Scale of River Difficulty. While often criticized for lacking precision and inviting subjective judgment, this scale re-

Downriver and whitewater training, including practice in eddy turns and other basic maneuvers, is offered by many Ohio paddling clubs. [ODNR photo]

mains the most widely recognized instrument for rating rivers. Paddlers should keep in mind, however, that one paddler's Class III may be another paddler's Class IV; the difficulty of a given river can change dramatically from day to day or even in the course of a few hours, when water levels can rapidly rise or fall.

International Scale of River Difficulty

If rapids on a river generally fit into one of the following classifications, but the water temperature is below 50°F or the trip is an extended one in a wilderness area, the river should be considered one class more difficult than normal.

Class I: Moving water with a few ripples and small waves; few or no obstructions

Class II: Easy rapids with waves up to 3 feet and wide, clear channels that are obvious without scouting; some maneuvering is required

Class III: Rapids with high, irregular waves often capable of swamping an open canoe; narrow passages that often require complex maneuvering; may require scouting from shore

Class IV: Long, difficult rapids with constricted passages that often require precise maneuvering in very turbulent waters. Scouting from shore is often necessary, and conditions make rescue difficult. Generally not possible for open canoes; boaters who venture onto Class IV: water in covered canoes and kayaks should be able to Eskimo roll.

Class V: Extremely difficult, long, and very violent rapids with highly congested routes that nearly always must be scouted from shore. Rescue conditions are difficult, and there is significant hazard to life in the event of a mishap. The ability to Eskimo roll is essential for kayakers and canoeists.

Class VI: Difficulties of Class V carried to the extremes of navigability; nearly impossible and very dangerous; for teams of experts only, after close study and with all precautions taken

American Whitewater Affiliation Safety Code

The American Whitewater Affiliation (AWWA) has published a safety code for paddlers. Although it touches on some of the same points made by the International Scale of River Difficulty, the code is printed in this book in its entirety because of its completeness and because the importance of its rules cannot be overstressed.

I. Personal Preparedness and Responsibility

A. **Be a competent swimmer** with the ability to handle yourself underwater.

B. **Wear a life jacket or other PFD.**

C. **Keep your craft under control.** Control must be good enough at all times to stop or reach shore before you reach any danger. Do not enter a rapid unless you are reasonably sure you can safely navigate it or swim the entire rapid in the event of capsize.

D. **Be aware of river hazards and avoid them.** Following are the most frequent killers.

   1. **High Water.** The river's power and danger and the difficulty of rescue increase tremendously as the flow rate increases. It is often misleading to judge river level at the put-in. Look at a narrow, critical passage. Could a sudden rise in the water level from sun on a snow pack, rain, or a dam release occur on your trip?

   2. **Cold.** Cold quickly robs your strength, along with your will and ability to save yourself. Dress to protect yourself from cold water and weather extremes. When the water temperature is less than 50°F, a diver's wet suit is essential for safety in event of an upset. Next best is wool clothing under a windproof outer garment such as a splashproof nylon shell; in this case one should carry matches and a complete change of clothes in a waterproof package. If after prolonged exposure a person experiences uncontrollable shaking or has difficulty talking and moving, he or she must be warmed immediately by whatever means available.

   3. **Strainers.** Brush, fallen trees, bridge pilings, or anything else that allows river current to sweep through but pins boat and boater against the obstacle. The water pressure on anything trapped this way is overwhelming, and there may be little or no white water to warn of this danger.

4. **Weirs, reversals, and souse holes.** Water drops over an obstacle, then curls back on itself in a stationary wave, as is often seen at weirs and dams. The surface water is actually going upstream, and this action will trap any floating object between the drop and the wave. Once trapped, a swimmer's only hope is to dive below the surface where current is flowing downstream or to try to swim out the end of the wave.

E. **Boating alone is not recommended**—the preferred minimum is three craft.

F. **Have a frank knowledge of your boating ability.** Don't attempt waters beyond this ability. Learn paddling skills and teamwork, if in a multiperson craft, to match the river you plan to boat.

G. **Be in good physical condition** consistent with the difficulties that may be expected.

H. **Be practiced in escape** from an overturned craft, in self-rescue, and in artificial respiration. Know first aid.

I. **The Eskimo roll should be mastered** by kayakers and canoeists planning to run large rivers or rivers with continuous rapids where a swimmer would have trouble reaching shore.

J. **Wear a crash helmet** where an upset is likely. This is essential in a kayak or covered canoe.

K. **Be suitably equipped.** Wear shoes that will protect your feet during a bad swim or a walk for help, yet will not interfere with swimming (tennis shoes recommended). Carry a knife and waterproof matches. If you need eyeglasses, tie them on and carry a spare pair. Do not wear bulky clothing that will interfere with your swimming when waterlogged.

II. Boat and Equipment Preparedness

A. **Test new and unfamiliar equipment** before relying on it for difficult runs.

B. **Be sure the craft is in good repair** before starting a trip. Eliminate sharp projections that could cause injury during a swim.

C. **Inflatable craft should have multiple air chambers** and should be test-inflated before starting a trip.

D. **Have strong, adequately sized paddles or oars** for controlling the craft and carry sufficient spares for the length of the trip.

E. **Install flotation devices** in noninflatable craft. These devices should be securely fixed and designed to displace as much water from the craft as possible.

F. **Be certain there is absolutely nothing to cause entanglement** when coming free from an upset craft; e.g., a spray skirt that won't release or that tangles around the legs; life jacket buckles or clothing that might snag; canoe seats that lock on shoe heels; foot braces that fail or allow feet to jam under them; flexible decks that collapse on boater's legs when trapped by water pressure; baggage that dangles in an upset; loose rope in the craft or badly secured bow and stern lines.

G. **Provide ropes to allow you to hold on to your craft** in case of upset and so that it may be rescued. Following are the recommended methods:

1. **Kayaks and covered canoes** should have 6-inch diameter grab loops of ½-inch rope attached to bow and stern. A stern painter 7 or 8 feet long is optional and may be used if properly secured to prevent entanglement.

2. **Open canoes** should have bow and stern lines (painters), securely attached, consisting of 8 to 10 feet of ½- or ⅜-inch rope. These lines must be secured in such a way that they will not come loose accidentally and entangle the boaters during a swim, yet they must be ready for immediate use during an emergency. Attached balls, floats, and knots are not recommended.

3. **Rafts and dories** should have taut perimeter grab lines threaded through the loops usually provided on the craft.

H. **Respect rules for craft capacity** and know how these capacities should be reduced for white-water use. (Life raft ratings must generally be halved.)

I. **Carry appropriate repair materials:** tape (heating-duct tape) for short trips, a complete repair kit for wilderness trips.

J. **Car-top racks must be strong and positively attached** to the vehicle, and each boat must be tied to each rack. In addition, each end of each boat should be tied to the car bumpers. Suction-cup racks are inadequate. The entire arrangement should be able to withstand all but the most violent accident.

III. Leader's Preparedness and Responsibility

A. **River Conditions.** Have a reasonable knowledge of the difficult parts of the run, or, if making an exploratory trip, examine maps to estimate the feasibility of the run. Be aware of possible rapid changes in river level and how these changes can affect the difficulty of the run. If important, determine approximate flow rate or level of the river. If the trip involves important tidal currents, secure tide information.

B. **Participants.** Inform participants of expected river conditions and determine whether the prospective boaters are qualified for the trip. All decisions should be based on group safety and comfort. Difficult decisions on the participation of marginal boaters must be based on group strength.

C. **Equipment.** Plan so that all necessary group equipment is present on the trip: 50- to 100-foot throwing rope, first aid kit with fresh and adequate supplies, extra paddles, repair materials, and survival equipment, if appropriate. Check equipment as necessary at the put-in, especially life jackets, boat flotation, and any items that could prevent complete escape from the boat in case of an upset.

D. **Organization.** Remind each member of individual responsibility in keeping the group compact and intact between the leader and the sweep (a capable rear boater). If the group is too large, divide into smaller groups, each of appropriate boating strength, and designate group leaders and sweeps.

E. **Float plan.** If your trip is into a wilderness area, or for an extended period, your plans should be filed with appropriate authorities or left with someone who will contact them after a certain time. Establishing checkpoints along the way from which civilization could be contacted if necessary should be considered; knowing the location of possible help could speed rescue in any case.

IV. In Case of Upset

A. **Evacuate your boat immediately** if there is imminent danger of being trapped against logs, brush, or any other form of strainer.

B. **Recover with an Eskimo roll** if possible.

C. **If you swim, hold on to your craft.** It has much flotation and is easy for rescuers to spot. Get to the upstream side of the craft so it cannot crush you against obstacles.

D. **Release your craft if this improves your safety.** If rescue is not imminent and water is numbingly cold, or if worse rapids follow, then strike out for the nearest shore.

E. **When swimming rocky rapids,** use backstroke with legs downstream and feet near the surface. If your foot wedges on the bottom, fast water will push you under and hold you there. Get to slow or very shallow water before trying to stand or walk. Look ahead. Avoid possible entrapment situations: rock wedges, fissures, strainers, brush, logs, weirs, reversals, and souse holes. Watch for eddies and slackwater so that you can be ready to use these when you approach. Use every opportunity to work your way to shore.

F. **If others spill, go after the boaters. Rescue boats and equipment only if this can be done safely.**

Knowing Your Rights on the River

In Ohio, a paddler's legal right to run a river or stream is based on the concept of navigability. The test is a simple one: if a stream is legally navigable, then the owners of adjoining property have no right to prohibit a paddler from running it; if a stream is not legally navigable, then the paddler has no right to run the stream without the permission of the adjoining landowners.

Unfortunately, while the test is simple, its implementation is not. Neither the Ohio legislature nor the Ohio courts has provided a list of rivers and streams that are considered legally navigable, although an act of the state legislature effective February 1988 empowered the director of natural resources to designate, mark, and map canoeing and boating routes with historic or scenic value. In addition to the director's power to expressly designate certain sections of river available for recreational use, paddlers can look to the state courts for a workable, although constantly evolving, definition of navigability.

Early in this century the legal definition of navigability centered on a river's capacity to support trade or commerce. In order to be considered navigable, a river had to have been capable of transporting the products of the country. In other words, it had to be fairly broad, deep, and slow with a more or less continuous channel—not particularly attractive from a paddler's standpoint. With the declining importance of river transportation and the increasing importance of recreational uses of the state's waterways, the Ohio courts' definition of navigability gradually changed. Currently, if a river or stream can be run by recreational paddlers irrespective of waterfalls, rapids, sandbars, shifting currents, or portages, then it is considered legally navigable and open to the public. However, the right of public use applies only to the water itself and not to the banks or even the stream bottom. Technically speaking, if a paddler steps out of his or her boat onto the stream bottom without permission, the paddler is trespassing.

The primary consideration in Ohio is not to identify the streams available for public recreational use but to discern the ways in which a paddler may get on them without trespassing. Of course, if a paddler obtains permission from a landowner, there is no problem. However, the owner of the appropriate parcel of streamside property must first be identified.

Access
The obvious solution to the problem of public use is public access points. The most common types of public access points, and the easiest to identify, are parks and bridges.

Public parks generally provide adequate parking for shuttle vehicles, offer some protection from vandalism, and provide the unquestioned right of public access. Often, however, the parks are not as conveniently located as paddlers would like, although the Ohio Department of Natural Resources (ODNR) has been very active in the last 10 years identifying and improving access sites for boaters.

Alternative access points—bridges—do not always have parking facilities or offer protection from vandalism, but they are more numerous than public parks and are often more conveniently located for the paddler. The primary problem with bridges is that the right of public access is not as clear as it is at public parks.

The right of public access evolves from the state's interest in the land under and around each bridge. This interest can take one of three forms.

1. The state can own the land outright, in which case the paddler's right of access is limited only by the state's power to regulate use of the land for the public benefit. For example, the state has the right to prohibit parking near the bridge if parked cars and pedestrian traffic in the vicinity of the bridge create a hazard for passing motorists or highway maintenance crews.

2. The state's interest can be classified as a right-of-way (or easement) for public transportation. In this case, the land under and around the bridge belongs to the adjacent landowners. The state (and thus the public) retains the right of access to the stream at the bridge as long as that access can be obtained without damaging the landowners' property (for example, bank erosion caused by putting in and taking out boats).

3. The state's interest can be classified as a limited-access easement (most common on, though not exclusive to, divided highways). Such an easement allows access only at designated points like on-ramps and does not provide a right of access for paddlers.

Assuming a paddler finds a conveniently located bridge, he or she is faced with the problem of determining the type of interest the state has in the adjacent property in order to determine the type of stream access the bridge affords. Unfortunately, short of a title search by a lawyer in the appropriate county recorder's office, there is no way to determine just which form the state's interest takes. However, certain assumptions can be safely made.

If the bridge is part of a divided highway with limited access, it can be safely assumed that the easement is a limited-access easement and that the paddler has no right of access to the stream at that point. It can also be assumed that there is no right of access where guardrails extend from either side of the bridge, making it impossible to safely park a shuttle vehicle, or where the physical characteristics of the streamside topography make it impossible to reach the water. Under no circumstances may a fence be crossed to gain access to a stream. Doing so would clearly be a trespassing violation, and the boater might be subject to civil or criminal prosecution.

If the roadway approaching the bridge or the terrain surrounding the bridge affords a place to park, if the stream is physically accessible, and if there are no fences to cross, it is probably safe to assume the right of access exists at that point. If you pick such a location to get on or off an Ohio stream and you are confronted by an angry landowner, be courteous, explain the situation, and apologize for any transgression (real or imagined) that you may have committed. You are probably within your legal rights, but you may be using a limited-access easement that doesn't look like a limited-access easement. Or you may have stumbled onto an easement where less careful paddlers or especially heavy use has created erosion problems. In any event, this is not the time to stand up for your rights. Remember, you could be wrong. In Ohio, if you trespass, you are liable for damages in a civil suit and may be found guilty of a criminal misdemeanor. Even if you're in the right, belligerent tactics on your part will only result in further damage to an already fragile relationship between landowners and paddlers.

By far the best tactic is one that is characterized by compromise and retreat. In Ohio a landowner has no right to detain you or make a citizen's arrest for trespassing. Only a police officer has the authority to take a trespasser into custody. Just walk away.

Streamside Rights

Regardless of the questions of navigability or public access, the right of landowners to prohibit trespassing on their land along streams is unquestioned. Paddlers are trespassing when they portage, camp, or even stop for a lunch break if they disembark from their boats onto privately owned land without permission.

When granting permission to cross or stop on private land, landowners extend a privilege that should be appreciated and respected. Do not betray a landowner's trust if you are extended the privilege of camping, putting in, or taking out. Do not litter, drive on grass or planted fields, or forget to close gates. In some cases property owners may resent people who drive for hundreds of miles to float through what the landowner may consider his or her private domain. Indeed, it is not unusual for landowners to firmly believe that they "own" the river or stream that passes through their land.

Good manners, appreciation, and consideration go a long way when approaching a landowner for permission to camp or launch. The property owner, who may be interested in paddling and flattered that the paddler is interested in the countryside, may also be quite friendly and approachable. Cultivate and value this friendship and avoid giving cause to deny paddlers access to the river at some future time.

Tips for Paddling with Kids

Paddling with children presents special opportunities for perceiving otherwise ordinary streamside encounters through a child's eye. But it also presents unique challenges lest that curiosity and enthusiasm become boredom or dread

Our travels have taught us 10 lessons about paddling with kids that might help make your first family trip a pleasant one.

Lesson 1. Before you put your children in a wiggly canoe on a moving stream, make sure they have had some time in the pool and have overcome their fear of water. Nothing dampens enthusiasm like a cold, wet dip in something they're afraid of anyway.

Lesson 2. Absolutely insist that your junior paddlers wear their PFDs at all times when on or near the water, and set a good example for them by wearing yours as well.

A kid-size paddle and a dip net: busy hands are happy hands.

Lesson 3. Teach and review basic safety lessons before every trip—the younger the child, the more basic and brief the lesson.

Lesson 4. Start with a short trip. It's almost impossible for the first one to be too short, and it's all too easy for it to be too long. Leave the kids hungry for more rather than sorry they came.

Lesson 5. Provide the children with a place to sit in the center of the canoe that is comfortable, dry, and low—floating cushions and booster seats work surprisingly well. An uncomfortable child is a squirmy one, and a squirmy child will rock your boat.

Lesson 6. Give each child a paddle, for the kids will want to be part of the action. Make it a small paddle with a small blade. They'll have an easier time handling it, and the small blade will keep them from working against you or having the paddle pulled from their hands.

Lesson 7. Take a dip net and small bucket so the kids can wade and catch critters in the riffles. This will add another dimension to their experience.

Lesson 8. Stop often so the children can get out and stretch, explore, wade, and dip.

Lesson 9. Pack food and drink. A hungry or thirsty child makes for a long trip, no matter how short the distance from put-in to take-out.

Lesson 10. Do not succumb to the temptation to throw in a fishing pole until your children have mastered the independent arts of angling and canoeing. One child strategically positioned in the middle of a 16-foot boat can reach every other paddler in the boat with the business end of a 6-foot fishing pole—and whether it actually happens or not, we guarantee that you will spend part of your time worrying about being hooked.

Ohio's Scenic Rivers Program

The Ohio Scenic Rivers Program (see Figure 2) was the first of its kind; it took effect in 1969, preceding even the federal scenic rivers program by several months. The Ohio Wild, Scenic, and Recreational Rivers Act gives the director of the ODNR "approval authority over public projects where building or enlargement of a highway, road, or structure or modification of the channel of any

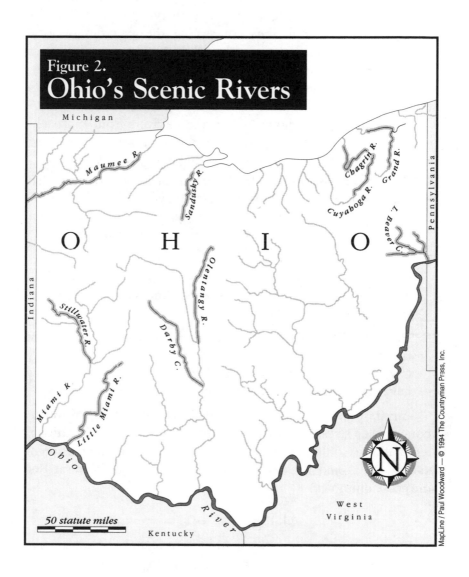

Figure 2.
Ohio's Scenic Rivers

Michigan

Maumee R.

Sandusky R.

Chagrin R.

Cuyahoga R.

Grand R.

L. Beaver C.

Pennsylvania

O H I O

Indiana

Olentangy R.

Stillwater R.

Darby C.

Miami R.

Little Miami R.

Ohio

River

West
Virginia

50 statute miles

Kentucky

watercourse takes place within the designated area." (This does not apply within the limits of municipal corporations.)

The rivers act stipulates that no strip-mining shall take place within 1,000 feet of a wild, scenic, or recreational river. While the act also involves stipulations concerning the activities of local landowners in designated areas, the ODNR makes every effort to acquire voluntary compliance by suggesting alternatives or compromises to construction plans or other uses of land that might affect a stream's scenic value or water quality.

The goal of the program is to preserve rivers from encroachment by civilization. Rivers, or, more accurately, sections of rivers, are designated according to the following categories:

A. "Wild river areas," to include those rivers or sections of rivers that are free of impoundments and generally inaccessible by trail, with watersheds or shorelines essentially primitive and water unpolluted, representing vestiges of primitive America

B. "Scenic river areas," to include those rivers or sections of rivers that are free of impoundments, with shoreline or watersheds still largely primitive and shorelines largely undeveloped but accessible in places by roads

C. "Recreational river areas," to include those rivers or sections of rivers that are readily accessible by road or railroad, that may have some development along their shorelines, and that may have undergone some impoundment or diversion in the past

Any responsible local organization can submit a petition to request that a stream be considered for wild, scenic, or recreational designation. (Contact the Ohio Scenic Rivers Program, Division of Natural Areas and Preserves, Ohio Department of Natural Resources, Columbus.)

Using This Book

Each stream description in this guide is accompanied by at least one map and a data table. Stream descriptions offer a primarily subjective reaction to each stream. They highlight points of interest, indicate sections that have been designated under the scenic rivers program, and convey a sense of the characteristics that make a given stream unlike any other in the state. Stream descriptions also indicate hazards that may appear on the streams to the extent that such hazards are predictable.

Maps

The maps in this book are not intended to replace topographic quadrangles for terrain features. Rather, they are intended to illustrate the general configuration of the stream, its access points, and the surrounding shuttle network of roads.

Futhermore, you may wish to consult more detailed county road maps when travelling to the access p;oints shown.

Data Tables

Data tables provide descriptive information along with information that is of a more quantitative or technical nature. Some of this information may also be discussed in the stream description for emphasis. Approximate river miles and car shuttle miles from one access point to the next are indicated on the tables. Table categories that require elaboration are discussed below.

USGS Quads: Names of United States Geological Survey (USGS) maps, listed under USGS Quads, facilitate the ordering or purchasing of maps from the USGS or from local dealers. Maps may be ordered from Division of Geological Survey, Ohio Department of Natural Resources, Fountain Square, Columbus, OH 43224, telephone (614) 466-5344.

Difficulty: Difficulty ratings (as discussed on page 18). A factor that must be kept in mind when considering this information is that difficulty often changes drastically with changing water levels. For example, an experienced beginner who successfully paddled White Oak Creek in Brown County at the minimum runnable water level (Class I), but who made the mistake of putting in on this stream as it approached flood stage (Class III–IV), is unlikely to get off the stream without injury to person or property. Unless otherwise stated, level of difficulty refers to normal conditions for each stream. Where two numbers are given, the first is an average, the second (in parentheses) pertains to the most difficult rapids on the stream under the most difficult conditions.

Hazards/Portages: Mandatory portages, such as dams, and more or less permanent hazards on the stream that may be portaged around are identified under Hazards/Portages. Changing water conditions and the presence of strainers and other unforeseen obstacles make it impossible to predict all the places that may require portaging. The burden of deciding when to portage is always on the paddler. It is the mark of a mature paddler to portage when in doubt.

Game-fish Species: Game fish that are known to be present in a given stream in significant numbers and that are frequently sought in that stream by local anglers are identified under Game-fish Species. Most Ohio streams contain populations of panfish, catfish, and carp, and you can assume these are present also, unless we have indicated otherwise.

Additional Info: Whenever possible, official agencies such as the Corps of Engineers, Ohio River Forecasters, and others who have access to gauges and can state river conditions precisely in cubic feet per second (cfs) or depth in feet are listed under Additional Info. Ohio River Forecasters can also provide forecasts for water levels for some streams. Sources also include canoe liveries, campgrounds, park rangers, and local inhabitants who have traditionally been happy to peer out their windows and tell curious paddlers how the river is running.

3

Streams of the Northwest

Two related factors figure prominently in the hydrology of north-western Ohio: the region is mostly flat and drainage is poor. Gradients of less than 1 foot per mile are not unusual in some areas, and in places there is not a hill—not even a dip or a swell—in sight. Travelers frequently remark on the unusual flatness of the area, which often brings to mind the bed of a huge lake. In fact, that is an accurate perception. Lake Erie, still gradually receding, once covered nearly the entire area. Much of the land now under cultivation consisted of dismal (from a farmer's point of view) swampland when the settlers arrived, and only intensive drainage efforts made the region habitable (for humans).

This is not to suggest that there is no white water in northwestern Ohio. Ironically, some of the best white water in the state is here. The Sandusky River, generally a well-behaved stream suitable for novice paddlers, offers some white water in the borderline Class IV range at high water levels. (One short section of the Sandusky River has been compared to Surprise!, a well-known rapid on the New River in West Virginia.) Even the Maumee River, which has a very low gradient on its western reaches, has one white-water stretch bordering on Class III when it's running high. Both streams resemble many eastern Lake Erie rivers—while overall gradient is low to moderate, the descent to lake level tends to occur in short, steep drops as opposed to being spread out evenly.

Still, these rivers are exceptions. And, to get back to the more typical features of northwestern Ohio, we kind of like swamps. Small parts of the fragile wetland ecology have been preserved around Lake Erie, most notably in preserves such as the Crane Creek Wildlife Sanctuary near Sandusky Bay. Whether the hard-fought battles of environmentalists to protect these delicate and rare ecosystems will come to naught remains to be seen. Apart from these preserves, however, most of the streams in the area share some marshland characteristics to some degree. If you're strictly a whitewater enthusiast, these streams offer little appeal. But if snaking silently through narrow channels of swamp grass past dense, mysterious bogs teeming with deer, raccoons, muskrats, waterfowl, hawks, and owls sounds interesting to you, northwestern Ohio has much to offer.

MAUMEE RIVER

The Maumee River offers an unusual kind of paddling for Ohio canoeists in the form of truly big water. From Defiance all the way down to Lake Erie, this broad, generally shallow river provides good paddling from ice-out in the early spring through autumn. The streambed, while rocky in places, affords little in the way of ledges or heavy rapids, but its gradient is sufficient to make paddling easy, especially at high water levels.

In Paulding and Defiance counties the Maumee winds through predominately agricultural surroundings consisting of broad, gently rolling plains. Farther east the hills increase in size, and the river flows through a wide floodplain. While the Maumee never strays far from civilization, long stretches of the river give paddlers a surprising sense of remoteness; even when bridges or cottages appear, the sheer size of the river seems to swallow them up. The huge sycamores, cottonwoods, and ashes lining the banks, and the black willows and marsh grasses poking up through the shallows, contribute to the unusual sense of vastness and isolation. Numerous wooded islands of all sizes add interest to the Maumee, and wildlife—

Co-author Combs and wife Claire paddle Maumee River, upstream from Farnsworth Metropark. [Jim Steiger photo]

including deer and especially waterfowl—is abundant, onshore as well as on the numerous islands.

One long set of shoals (about 100 yards long) on the Maumee brings out local white-water enthusiasts from the Toledo area when the river is running high. Referred to as Turkey Foot Rapids, these shoals, a short distance upstream from the I-475 bridge, provide good open-boat rapids approaching the Class III range when the depth gauge under the bridge reads 572–573, mainly in the form of boat-swamping waves, ledges, and rollers. As water levels reach 574 on the gauge, these rapids tend to wash out. The lack of undercut rocks and keeper hydraulics makes these rapids good white-water practice for advanced-beginner and intermediate paddlers.

Access on the Maumee from Defiance to Toledo is excellent. Camping is available on the river at Farnsworth Metropark, about 8 miles downstream from the Grand Rapids dam, on river left opposite the very large Missionary Island. Camping is primitive, and there is a fee of several dollars.

If you're a history buff, the Maumee has much to recommend it. Roche de Boeuf, a huge limestone escarpment overlooking the river

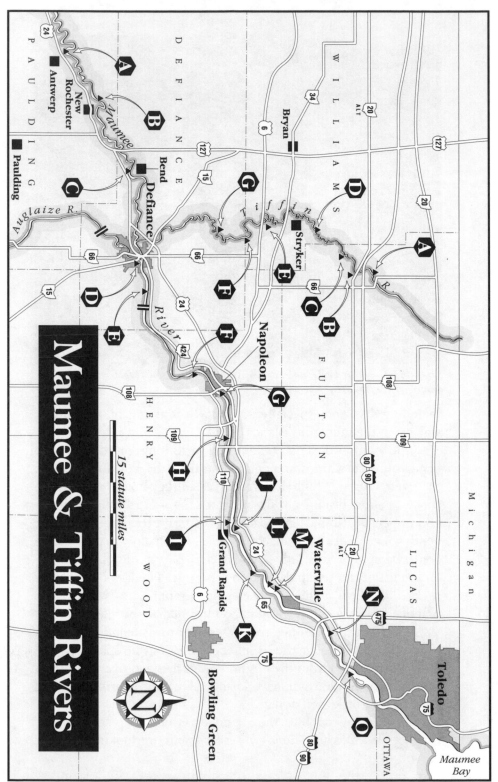

Maumee & Tiffin Rivers

15 statute miles

near the monolithic ruins of the Waterville Electric bridge and the Farnsworth Metropark, was the meeting place of Little Turtle, Blue Jacket, Tarhe the Crane, and other Native Americans making plans to defeat the army of Anthony Wayne and several generals before him. The Battle of Fallen Timbers (1794) occurred very close to Side Cut Park, and several forts, including Fort Deposit, were located along the river in this area. (For more information on local Native American lore and pioneer history, including the sites of forts, trails, and restored sawmills, gristmills, and so forth, write to the Maumee Valley Historical Society, 1031 River Road, Maumee, OH 43573, or call (419) 893-9602.)

There are several obstacles on this Class I river, including large (but easily portaged) power dams east of Defiance and Grand Rapids. You're also likely to find many anglers on the Maumee. Fishing is excellent here, especially as the river approaches Lake Erie and particularly from late March to early May, when the annual walleye spawning run brings out anglers in droves with hip waders and johnboats. Respect their right to use the river, steer clear of them, and paddle by as quickly and unobtrusively as possible, unless you want to bring a rod and reel and get in on the action yourself.

Maumee River

Counties:	Paulding, Defiance, Henry, Wood, Lucas
USGS Quads:	Woodburn North (IN), Antwerp, Paulding, Sherwood, Defiance West, Defiance East, Florida, Napoleon West, Colton, Grand Rapids, Bowling Green North, Maumee, Rossford, Toledo, Oregon
Difficulty:	International Class I
Hazards/Portages:	Dams at Defiance, Grand Rapids
Game-fish Species:	Walleye, smallmouth bass
Additional Info:	Independence Dam State Park (419) 784-3263

Access Point	Section	River Miles	Shuttle Miles
A. Antwerp Park off US 24 in Antwerp	A–B	8	7
B. Access off Township Rd. 226 W of New Rochester	B–C	12	12.5
C. Access off Bend Rd. bridge S of Bend	C–D	12	11
D. Kingsbury Park off Front St. in Defiance	D–E	3	3
E. Independence Dam State Park off OH 424 (access below dam, too)	E–F	12.5	12
F. Access off OH 424 SW of Napoleon	F–G	3	3
G. Ritter Park off Riverview Dr. in Napoleon	G–H	5	5
H. Access off OH 24 before OH 109N	H–I	8	8.5
I, J. Providence and Thurston parks on opposite banks in Grand Rapids	I, J–K	6	5
K. Ostego Park off OH 65 in Ostego	K–L	2	1
L. Access Range Line Rd. off OH 65 N of Ostego, river right	L–M	2.5	7.5
M. Farnsworth Park SW of Waterville off OH 24	M–N	7	8
N. Side Cut Metropark off South River Rd. SW of Maumee, river left	N–O	7	9
O. International Park off Cherry St., in Toledo, public docks			

AUGLAIZE RIVER

The headwaters of the Auglaize River come together in Putnam County and flow south into Auglaize County. In Wapakoneta the stream nearly doubles back on itself and turns north, draining parts of Putnam, Paulding, and Defiance counties before emptying into the Maumee at Defiance. From Wapakoneta north into Putnam County, the Auglaize is a small, serpentine stream winding its way slowly through a narrow floodplain so dense with undergrowth in places that visibility is limited to a few feet. The streambed is generally soft and marshy, and the river varies in width from 15 to 80 or more feet; where the river is wide and shallow it is nearly choked with vegetation, with only two or three narrow channels snaking through the swamp grass.

There are a lot of sandbars and mud flats in this region, and the river forks frequently around tiny islands. Logjams are numerous in spots; some are as big as houses, backing water up behind them like beaver dams, and portaging can necessitate a little bushwhacking. Spring is the best time to paddle the Auglaize, because despite the efforts of local paddlers to keep the stream open, after July 1 the Auglaize County section of the river is apt to be so weed-choked in places it becomes unnavigable. High water eliminates this problem but increases the nuisance posed by strainers.

If you paddle quietly on this part of the Auglaize, you will discover that wildlife—particularly waterfowl—is abundant, and you'll probably get a very close look at a great blue heron before it goes lumbering off over the marsh like something out of Lost World. It's not at all unusual, where visibility permits, to see owls flying about in the middle of the day, adding to an air of mystery on this section of the river. While the Auglaize is hardly remote, the numerous small bridges that cross the stream and the occasional farmhouse or barn along the bank is quickly swallowed up in the undergrowth and lost to sight and mind.

In Putnam County the terrain flattens out, and the undergrowth gives way to open farm country. The river follows a straight course and has been dredged in places. The banks are open and muddy, and, generally speaking, the farther downstream you get, the less interesting the Auglaize becomes. A huge power dam south of Defiance backs the river up into a *reservoir* with a lot of powerboat traffic. From the dam it's only a few miles to the confluence with the Maumee.

Auglaize River

Counties:	Auglaize, Allen, Putnam, Paulding, Defiance
USGS Quads:	Wapakoneta, Moulton, Spencerville, Delphos, Ottoville, Kalida, Continental
Difficulty:	International Class I
Hazards/Portages:	Logjams, dam south of Defiance
Game-fish Species:	Smallmouth bass
Additional Info:	Fort Amanda Livery in Cridersville (419) 657-6782

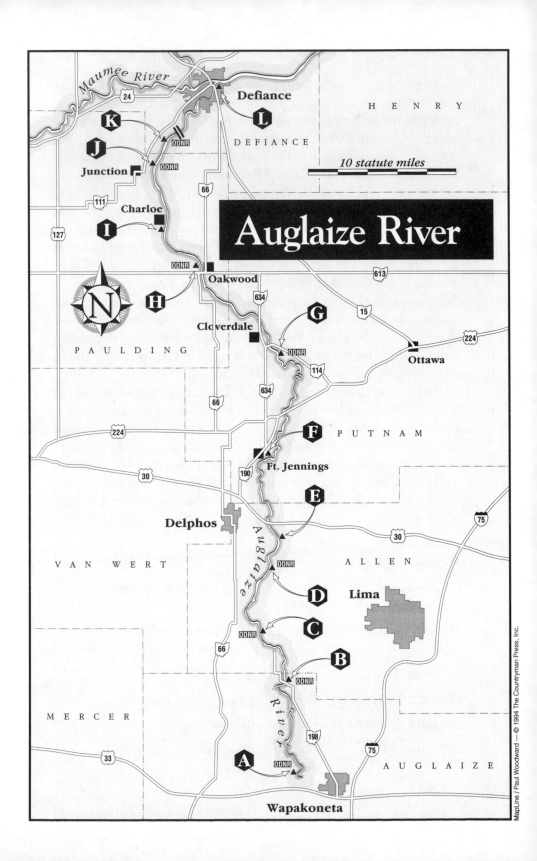

Access Point	Section	River Miles	Shuttle Miles
A. Glynwood Rd. bridge NW of Wapakoneta	A–B	8	6
B. OH 198 SE of Spencerville across from Ft. Amanda Livery	B–C	6	6
C. Agerter Rd. bridge	C–D	6	6
D. Piquad Rd. bridge	D–E	4	5
E. Ridge Rd. bridge	E–F	7.5	5
F. Park off OH 190 in Ft. Jennings	F–G	14	11
G. Rest stop at OH 634 and OH 114 E of Cloverdale	G–H	8.5	10
H. Oakwood City Park off Cook St. and OH 66 in Oakwood	H–I	4	5
I. County Rd. 138 bridge in Charloe	I–J	5.5	6
J. OH 111 bridge N of Junction	J–K	3	3
K. Access at dam upstream of Power Dam Rd. bridge	K–L	6	5
L. Kingsbury Park in Defiance off Second St. at mouth of river			

BLANCHARD RIVER

The Blanchard River is *the* old millstream. Tell Taylor composed his famous song "Down by the Old Mill Stream" while fishing along the Blanchard a few miles upstream from Findlay in 1908. Unfortunately for the burgeoning numbers of paddlers who happen to also be barbershop quartet fans, this stretch of river offers seasonal paddling at best, except for the water backed up behind the dam at Riverside Park.

Your best bet is to put in downstream from Findlay. There are several good access points between the Liberty Landing and the confluence with the Auglaize south of Dupont—not so many, however, as to spoil the scenery. Thanks primarily to the efforts of the Hancock Park District and local paddlers, the Blanchard retains most of its rustic charm.

From Findlay to Ottawa, the Blanchard meanders through fairly flat farm country and woodlots, with densely vegetated banks and trees leaning into the river. There are enough turns and riffles to keep you awake, and at high water levels, when the current is faster, frequent deadfalls can present a hazard for the inexperienced.

Six miles downstream from the access at County Road 53 is Blanchard River Village (Gilboa), a restored mid-1800s river town that is a good stopover for anyone interested in the history of the area.

Just upstream from Ottawa, after the Buckeye Sugar Mill Dam, the Blanchard becomes noticeably narrower and a little faster. (The dam is very small and can be easily run at low water levels, or it can be easily portaged.) The terrain changes from predominately flat farmland to rolling, more wooded hills,

A solid low brace keeps this young kayaker from an upsetting lesson.

and the banks on this part of the stream range from 4 to 30 or 40 feet in height. The occasional deep gullies, sharp turns, and increased likelihood of deadfalls across the stream (due in part to the narrowness of this stretch of the Blanchard) make this part of the river potentially hazardous at high water levels.

Blanchard River

Counties:	Hancock, Putnam
USGS Quads:	Findlay, McComb, Leipsic, Ottawa, Miller City, Continental
Difficulty:	International Class I
Hazards/Portages:	Strainers, infrequent logjams
Game-fish Species:	Smallmouth bass
Additional Info:	Millstream Canoe Livery (419) 422-1433 or 422-7148

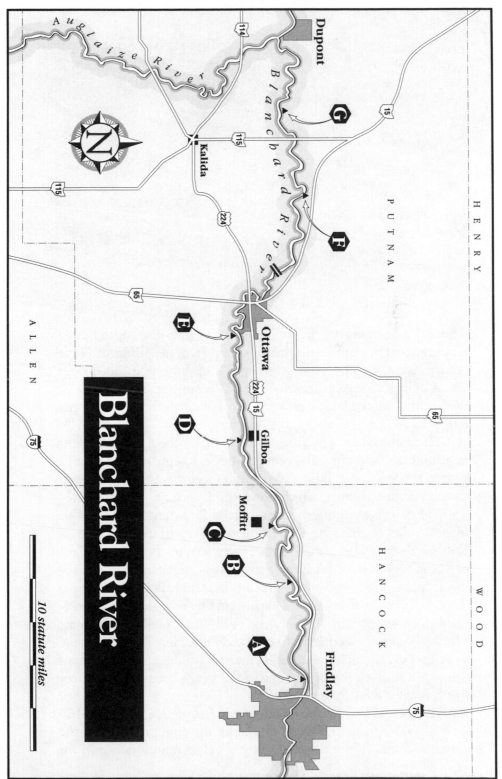

Blanchard River

10 statute miles

Access Point	Section	River Miles	Shuttle Miles
A. Liberty Landing access off junction of Liberty Township Rd. 89 and County Rd. 140 W of Findlay	A–B	7	6
B. Blanchard Landing access off OH 235 bridge W of Findlay	B–C	4.5	5
C. Bridge at County Rd. 53 N of Moffit	C–D	5	6
D. Fire Pump Landing in Gilboa off Old OH 224	D–E	7.5	6
E. Old OH 224 access E of Ottawa	E–F	11.5	8.5
F. Bridge at Township Rd. 205	F–G	7	5
G. County Rd. 21 E of Dupont			

TIFFIN RIVER

The Tiffin River begins, depending on which map you use, in Fulton County about three miles northeast of Stryker, or in Michigan. Three streams come together near Stryker. The center one is called Bean Creek by locals and comes down out of Michigan. Some maps make no distinction between Bean Creek and the Tiffin, referring to the entire length as the Tiffin River.

The Tiffin is one of two major streams in northern Ohio that flow in a southerly direction. The other is the St. Joseph, which follows a course parallel to the Tiffin, 20–30 miles to the west. Both streams empty into the Maumee, which flows into Lake Erie.

The two rivers are quite similar, but the Tiffin tends to run slightly bigger and through a somewhat more varied topography than the St. Joe. Northern reaches of this river are pretty in spots, but some sections of Bean Creek near Michigan appear to have been channelized, flowing in a straight line through nearly treeless farmland. This section of the river is shallow, with occasional logjams in the few spots that are tree-lined. Downstream from the Ohio Turnpike is Goll Woods State Nature Preserve, a section well worth paddling. Here Bean Creek and two other streams flow together in a maze of winding, marshy streams through a small virgin forest—one of the state's last stands of timber that has never seen a saw or an ax.

The river widens considerably at this point, varying from 50 to 100 feet in width, and the gradient picks up enough to keep the current moving, if not always quickly. Terrain is unusually hilly for northern Ohio from this point on down to the Maumee, and the river flows between high banks, 50 feet or more in places. Surroundings alternate between hardwood forest and open farmland. Water quality on the Tiffin, as on the St. Joe, is excellent.

Several landowners on the southern stretches of the Tiffin have requested and been granted permission from the state to channelize some sections of the river in an effort to control erosion, which is a problem in this area. Despite some channelization, the Tiffin remains for the most part in a natural condition. (A map of the Tiffin River is on page 36.)

Tiffin River

Counties:	Fulton, Williams, Defiance
USGS Quads:	Fayette, Archbold, West Unity, Evansport, Defiance West
Difficulty:	International Class I
Hazards/Portages:	Strainers, logjams
Game-fish Species:	Smallmouth bass

Access Point	Section	River Miles	Shuttle Miles
A. Southern Rd. bridge off OH 66, 5 mi. S of Fayette	A–B	3	2
B. Access off Copeland-Corners Rd. bridge NW of Archbold	B–C	2	2
C. Short Goll Rd. bridge	C–D	6	6
D. Access off OH 2	D–E	9	6
E. County Rd. C, S of Stryker	E–F	4	4
F. Williams-Defiance County Line Rd.	F–G	12	8
G. Stever Rd. bridge NW of Brunersburg			

ST. JOSEPH RIVER

The St. Joseph River begins in the northwest corner of the state near the small town of Pioneer in Williams County. It winds its way south through flat to gently rolling, marshy terrain to cut through a corner of Defiance County before entering Indiana, where it empties into the Maumee in Fort Wayne. The St. Joseph is small but usually navigable year-round. Surrounding countryside is for the most part open farmland, but the river itself is tree-lined and flows through small groves of hardwoods. Wildlife—especially waterfowl and small mammals such as muskrats and raccoons—is plentiful, and quiet paddlers frequently spot deer along the river. The low volume of water, together with occasional strainers or logjams, make it possible that you'll have to do a little walking on this stream. Current ranges from nearly slack to fairly quick in sections where the gradient is a little steeper. Camping is available at a riverside campground near Pioneer. The river opens up considerably, becoming 80–100 feet wide near the Williams–Defiance county line, where the terrain becomes abruptly hillier. Although the St. Joe rarely strays far from country roads, the area is sparsely settled by Ohio standards. Water quality is quite good.

St. Joseph River

Counties:	Williams, Defiance
USGS Quads:	Pioneer, Montpelier, Blakeslee, Edgerton
Difficulty:	International Class I
Hazards/Portages:	Strainers

Paddling can get you to largemouth-bass water that gets little pressure from other Ohio anglers.

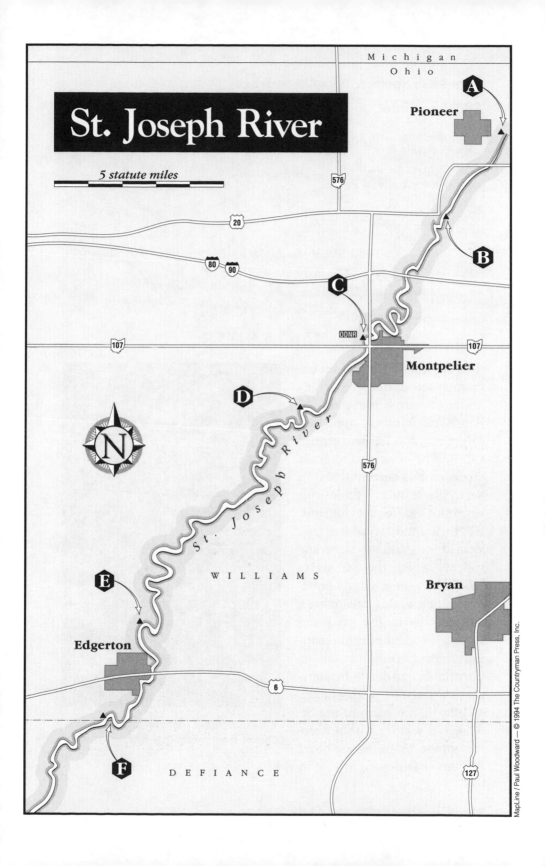

St. Joseph River

5 statute miles

Game-fish Species: Smallmouth bass

Additional Info: Lazy River Campground (419) 485-4411

Access Point	Section	River Miles	Shuttle Miles
A. County Rd. R, E of Pioneer	A–B	3.5	4
B. OH 20 SW of Pioneer	B–C	8	7
C. Williams County Fair Grounds in Montpelier off OH 107	C–D	4	4.5
D. County Rd. 18 bridge SW of Montpelier	D–E	11	9.5
E. County Rd. J, NE of Edgerton	E–F	8	6
F. Williams-Defiance County Line Rd.			

ST. MARYS RIVER

The St. Marys River is an extremely serpentine stream meandering across the plains of Auglaize, Mercer, and Van Wert counties in west-central Ohio. For many paddlers a stream with a current that is in many places indiscernible, with no rapids and frequent logjams, has little appeal. And it is true that if its gradient were any more gradual, the St. Marys would be a long, skinny pond. Nonetheless, this stream has a singular charm: it is small and intimate, tucked away in a channel winding through woodlots, cornfields, and dense, mysterious bogs teeming with wildlife. While hardly remote, the St. Marys is seldom within hearing range of traffic or other human activities.

A Class II rapids, like those on many Ohio streams, provides an ideal spot for this youngster to practice his downriver skills.

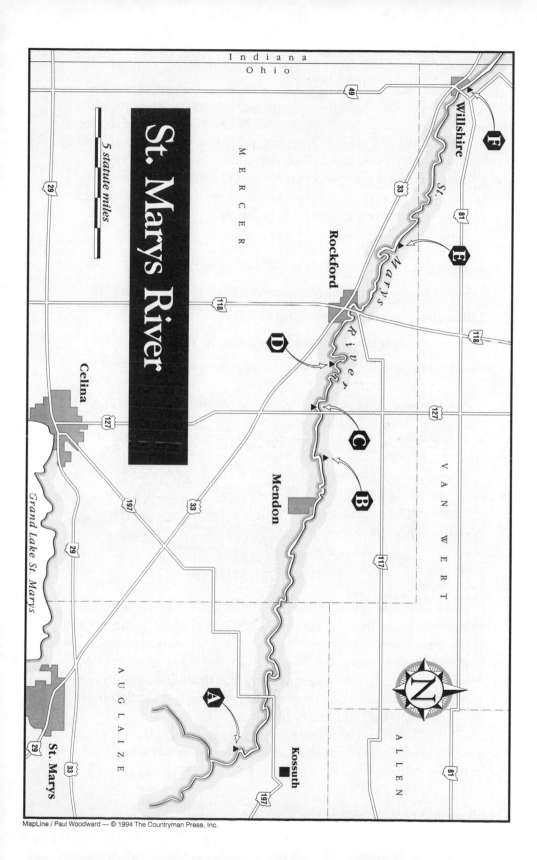

St. Marys River

5 statute miles

Public access is limited on the first section of the stream, although you may be able to obtain permission from private land-owners to get on the water somewhere between the first and second accesses indicated on our map. Be prepared to portage around numerous logjams on this stream, depending on the time of year you paddle it. If and when you portage, avoid causing erosion problems to private property that could result in sections of this stream becoming effectively off-limits to paddlers.

St. Marys River

Counties: Auglaize, Mercer, Van Wert

USGS Quads: Elgin, Mendon, Rockford, Willshire (IN)

Difficulty: International Class I

Hazards/Portages: Logjams, rock dam in Willshire

Game-fish Species: Smallmouth bass

Access Point	Section	River Miles	Shuttle Miles
A. Barber-Werner Rd. bridge S of Kossuth	A–B	16	14
B. Palmer Rd. bridge W of Mendon	B–C	2	2
C. Access off US 127	C–D	3	4
D. Frysinger Rd. bridge	D–E	7	10
E. Township Line Rd. bridge	E–F	8	8
F. OH 81/49 bridge in Willshire			

PORTAGE RIVER

If you are familiar with the Mad, the Whitewater, and the Stillwater, you might guess that the Portage is a river on which portaging is never necessary. Wrong. The Portage River is aptly named: paddle this river in the summer, and you'll most likely do a lot of walking. From ice-out in late February or early March to May, the Portage can provide a scenic cruise through the farmland and small towns of Wood, Sandusky, and Ottawa counties.

Several dredged, treeless, and possibly canoeable but generally uninteresting forks of the Portage come together near New Rochester. From this point downstream, the river is typically broad and

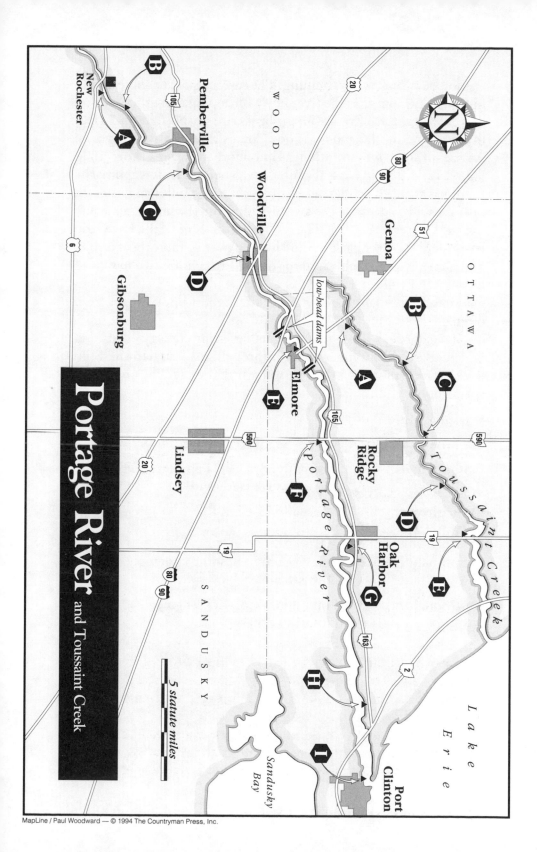

Portage River and Toussaint Creek

New Rochester

Pemberville

U.S. 105

W O O D

Woodville

U.S. 6

Gibsonburg

Genoa

U.S. 20

U.S. 80 90

U.S. 51

O T T A W A

low-head dams

Elmore

U.S. 590

Lindsey

U.S. 20

U.S. 105

Rocky Ridge

Portage River

T o u s s a i n t   C r e e k

U.S. 590

U.S. 19

Oak Harbor

S A N D U S K Y

U.S. 19

U.S. 80 90

U.S. 163

U.S. 2

Port Clinton

L a k e   E r i e

Sandusky Bay

5 statute miles

shallow but usually clear-running. The current quickens perceptibly in Sandusky County as the river begins dropping more steeply in its descent to the Lake Erie basin; the banks rise steeply to 20 or 30 feet in places, and the flatlands of Wood County give way to rolling hills. A series of small limestone ledges in Elmore provides a short (100–200 yards) stretch of Class II white water when the river is approaching flood stage. A similar series of ledges a few miles downstream near the OH 590 bridge can also provide Class II white water at just the right water levels. Oak Harbor marks the edge of the Lake Erie basin; here the river backs up and is taken over by motorboat traffic.

The only predictable hazards on the Portage are two low-head dams near Elmore. The first is a very small dam upstream from Elmore; the second, slightly larger dam is just downstream from town.

The Portage River seldom gets far from country roads and farmhouses, and it frequently flows through small rural towns. Still, it's a clear, clean-running stream well worth the paddling on a sunny spring day.

Portage River

Counties: Wood, Sandusky, Ottawa

USGS Quads: Jerry City, Bradner, Pemberville, Elmore, Lindsey, Oak Harbor

Difficulty: International Class I

Hazards/Portages: Low-head dams in Elmore

Game-fish Species: Smallmouth bass, some largemouth bass downstream

Additional Info: Huntington Corps of Engineers (304) 529-5604

Access Point	Section	River Miles	Shuttle Miles
A. Zepernick Rd. bridge	A–B	2	2
B. Wayne Rd. bridge	B–C	4	4
C. Bradner Rd. bridge E of Pemberville	C–D	6.6	6
D. Trailmarker Park off Cherry St. in Woodville	D–E	6	4

E. OH 51 bridge in Elmore	E–F	6	4
F. OH 590 bridge	F–G	4.5	4.5
G. OH 163 in Oak Harbor	G–H	8	6
H. ODNR access off OH 163	H–I	3	5
I. Waterworks Park off Jefferson St. in Port Clinton			

TOUSSAINT CREEK

Toussaint Creek is similar to many streams in northwestern Ohio and interesting for the same reason that many other streams in the area are interesting: its fragile marshland ecology. The Toussaint begins as far south as Bowling Green, where it is hardly more than a drainage ditch. Not until it reaches Ottawa County does the Toussaint become more than marginally navigable, and even in Ottawa County logjams and thick vegetation can present problems until as far downstream as Benton-Carroll Road. Here the gradient, low prior to this point, becomes almost nonexistent as the Toussaint approaches Lake Erie, and the stream widens to enter a flat, marshy area typical of the western Lake Erie basin, teeming with waterfowl and other wildlife. This lower section of the stream (if you can call it a stream at this point) has a strange, mysterious quality common to the Lake Erie wetlands.

From Benton-Carroll Road, the current on the Toussaint is slack, making it possible to explore the area and return easily to the point of departure—or you can continue on "downstream" to the Toussaint Creek Wildlife Area or Lake Erie.

Toussaint Creek

Counties: Ottawa

USGS Quads: Genoa, Oak Harbor, Lacarne

Difficulty: International Class I

Hazards/Portages: None

Game-fish Species: Smallmouth bass, largemouth bass in
                        backwaters, irregular spring walleye run

Additional Info: Resthaven/Toussaint Creek Wildlife Area
                        (419) 684-5049

Access Point	Section	River Miles	Shuttle Miles
A. Fulkert Rd. bridge	A–B	4.5	4
B. Elliston-Trowbridge Rd. bridge	B–C	4	3
C. OH 590 bridge	C–D	4.5	3
D. Benton-Carroll Rd. bridge	D–E	4.5	3
E. Toussaint Creek Wildlife Area OH 19			

SANDUSKY RIVER

The Sandusky River starts as a brook near Crestline in Crawford County. From there it twists its way through hills that rise and dip like swells on the ocean, past Bucyrus, slowly picking up steam but still hardly more than a trickle, and into Wyandot County. Here it turns north, and not until it reaches Upper Sandusky is the river more than a wet-weather stream. From Upper Sandusky to Roger Young Memorial Park in Fremont (Sandusky County), the Sandusky is designated a state scenic river.

The Sandusky flows over a dolomite and limestone bed (silted over in places). Terrain is typical of northern Ohio, alternating between flat bottomland and rolling, broken ridges characteristic of end moraines deposited by glaciers. Exceptions to this are the area

The hydraulic below a midstream ledge offers an Ohio kayaker a place to practice her surfing technique.

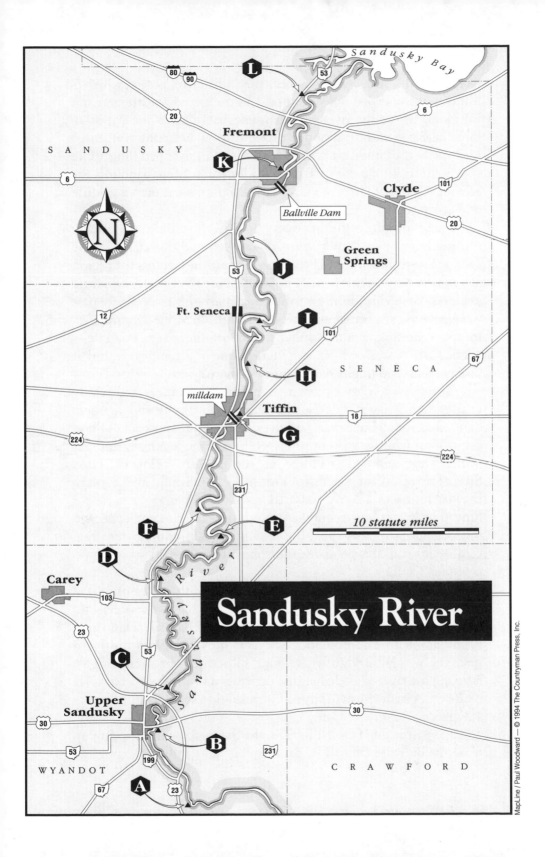

Sandusky River

just north of Upper Sandusky near the Indian Mill access, which is hillier and somewhat more rugged, and the area downstream from Fremont, where the river broadens and backs up in the flat-as-a-table lake basin. The area downstream from Fremont is open to motorboat traffic and is closer to flatwater than river paddling. (The south shore of Sandusky Bay provides interesting paddling for anyone who wants to explore wetlands and examine marsh wildlife and ecosystems.)

Those paddling the Sandusky for the first time are usually pleasantly surprised by a sense of remoteness, especially in the section between Tiffin and Fremont. Despite the fact that the region around the Sandusky is heavily populated, the river itself bears little evidence of civilization. For the most part the river flows past wooded banks and occasional fields, with high limestone outcroppings in spots along the northern one-third of the river. Wildlife—particularly waterfowl—is abundant along the Sandusky, and if you're lucky you might see a bald eagle here.

Generally a Class I stream suitable for beginners and family cruises, at high water levels the Sandusky is swift and in spots dangerous for all but expert paddlers. As the river approaches flood stage, local white-water enthusiasts head for the Sandusky and put in below the milldam in Tiffin. Just downstream, below the Huss Street bridge, are the remains of a washed-out old milldam that mark the beginning of a lively Class III rapids consisting of a series of limestone ledges and hydraulics. Exercise caution as you approach the beginning of this run—the undercut rocks and twisted steel reinforcing rods that comprise the remnants of the dam make this no place for a spill.

White-water paddlers frequently take out at the County Road 38 bridge; after this the gradient levels off and the river is deep and comparatively slow all the way down to the Ballville Dam near Fremont—with one exception. Several hundred yards upstream from the Tyndall Bridge, where King's Rock juts out on river right, is an almost river-wide ledge that provides a taste of solid Class III white water in the form of large haystacks and a sharp drop. (There's a bypass chute on river left.)

Soon after the Tyndall Bridge, the Sandusky starts backing up from the Ballville Dam. The dam itself is quite difficult to portage (although Dick Teeple of the notorious Toledo River Gang claims to have done so by lowering canoes over the wall by rope on river right and climbing down after them). In any case, this dam is dangerous and has been declared off-limits. We recommend taking out at Chief Tarhe Park.

The best white water on the Sandusky (at high water levels) is below the Ballville Dam. This is primarily decked-boat water (borderline Class IV) and should be scouted carefully. Paddlers generally put in on river left below the dam, opposite steep limestone bluffs. Immediately downstream, notice two islands near the center of the stream. The channel to the left of the islands is marked at high water by large standing waves, a sharp ledge, and two nasty hydraulics. They're stoppers, so punch them hard if you run this channel. You can slip by the hydraulics by ferrying quickly toward the center of the river, hugging the left side of the first island, and eddying-out behind it. From there you can peel out and work your way around the right side of the second island.

About a quarter mile downstream is a hydroplant where you can take out or, if you're feeling cocky and ready for more Class IV white water, you can continue on downstream a short distance to the golf course on river left. After you wipe out in the high standing waves and rescue operations are complete, you can drag your kayak ashore and take up golf.

Sandusky River

Counties:	Wyandot, Seneca, Sandusky
USGS Quads:	Nevada, Upper Sandusky, McCutchenville, Tiffin South, Tiffin North, Fremont West, Fremont East
Difficulty:	International Class I (several Class III and IV areas at high water levels)
Hazards/Portages:	Dams, logjams (especially in Wyandot County)
Game-fish Species:	Walleye, smallmouth bass
Additional Info:	Portage Trail Canoe Livery in Fremont (419) 334-2988

Access Point	Section	River Miles	Shuttle Miles
A. Township Rd. 124 A bridge E of Harpster	A–B	8.5	9
B. Harrison Smith Park off US 30 in Upper Sandusky	B–C	6	5
C. Indian Mill Park off OH 23/ County Rd. 47G	C–D	10	11
D. County Rd. 16 bridge	D–E	11	8
E. ODNR access off Pennington Rd. bridge	E–F	4	4
F. Bridge off County Rd. 6	F–G	9.5	9
G. Access at Water St. N of Huss St. bridge in Tiffin	G–H	5	4
H. County Rd. 38 bridge and County Rd. 33 N of Tiffin	H–I	6	4
I. County Rd. 33 bridge NE of Ft. Seneca	I–J	9	7
J. Wolf Creek Park off OH 53 S of Fremont	J–K	7	6
K. Roger Young Park off Front St. in Fremont	K–L	9.5	6
L. Dempsey Sandusky Bay Public Access off Bayshore Dr. 12 mi. N of river mouth on Sandusky Bay			

4

Streams of the Northeast

Streams in the northeast part of the state follow a common pattern: they have their headwaters in the Glaciated Appalachian Plateau where they develop as woodland streams with little gradient, frequently flowing through marshlands where drainage is poor. Several streams initially flow southward in a sort of confused search for the lower level of Lake Erie before finally turning northward to begin their pursuit in earnest.

While Ohio is certainly not known for its white water, a good portion of what there is lies in this area. As streams of this region approach the lake and begin to slice down through the strata toward the level of the Lake Plains, their valleys get narrower and deeper and gradient becomes more noticeable, often exhibiting itself in abrupt drops over bedrock ledges. Most of these ledges are small, ranging from a few inches to a few feet. Some of them, however, are severe, like the matched falls on the East and West branches of the Black River or the Sandstone Falls of the Rocky River or the Cuyahoga Falls on the Cuyahoga. The falls make the northeast perhaps the most attractive part of the state for white-water enthusiasts. They can choose from the steady Class IIs characteristic of the Ashtabula and Conneaut or the short but intense Class IIIs and IVs of the Lower Gorge on the Cuyahoga or Tinkers Creek.

VERMILION RIVER

The Vermilion River is among northern Ohio's most beautiful streams, winding through rugged, grandiose hills in Huron, Lorain, and Erie counties before emptying into Lake Erie. Steep bluffs ranging from 100 to 200 feet and higher border the river on some stretches (particularly in the central sections). The rugged terrain in the immediate vicinity of the Vermilion allows for only small, scattered farms; hardwood forests, with occasional stands of evergreen, cover the surrounding hills.

The regular gradient of the stream affords little in the way of sharp drops or true white water, but it is

A quick draw stroke can keep a solo paddler from being swept into the bank.

steep enough to keep paddlers moving along at a good clip. From Fitchville downstream toward Wakeman, the Vermilion provides enjoyable paddling in early spring and following prolonged or heavy spells of rain in summer. Surrounding countryside on this section tends to be more pastoral and a little less rugged than farther downstream, and the river flows through a somewhat wider floodplain, with small farms and thick second-growth woodlots predominating. As the Vermilion passes through Wakeman and on into Erie County, the continued influx of tributaries increases its volume to provide almost year-round

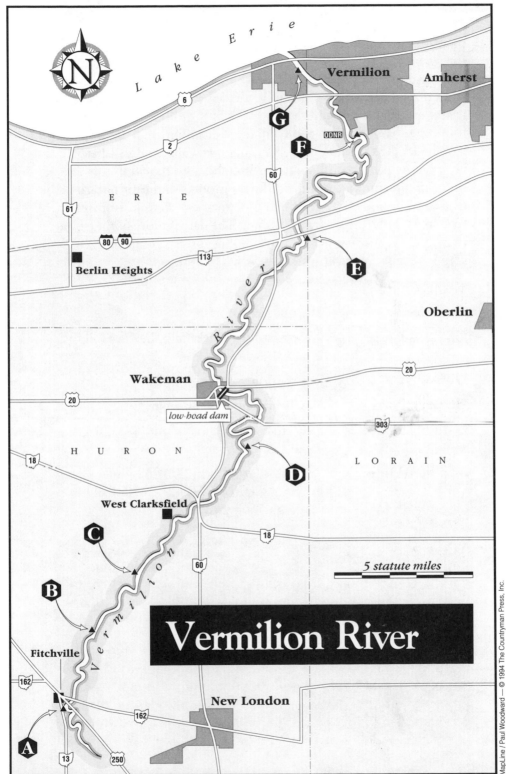

Vermilion River

5 statute miles

paddling. From Wakeman to Mill Hollow–Bacon Woods Park in Lorain County is the more rugged and perhaps (depending on your taste) most beautiful section of the Vermilion. Downstream from the park the river tends to get wider, flatter, and shallower as it approaches Lake Erie.

Access is generally good on the Vermilion, making trips of varying lengths possible. The Vermilion is wide enough—particularly on the central and northern stretches—to moderate the nuisance of logjams and strainers. There is one significant hazard on this Class I+ stream in the form of a low-head dam just upstream from the OH 60 bridge in Wakeman. The dam is more bothersome than most because it is hard to portage, but you can get around it with some difficulty on river left.

Vermilion River

Counties:	Huron, Erie, Lorain
USGS Quads:	New London, Clarksfield, Berlin Heights, Kipton, Vermilion East
Difficulty:	International Class I+
Hazards/Portages:	Lowhead dam in Wakeman
Game-fish Species:	Largemouth and smallmouth bass; seasonal steelhead run
Additional Info:	Romp's Water Port (216) 967-4342; River Forecast Center (513) 421-3670, daily readings not available

Access Point	Section	River Miles	Shuttle Miles
A. US 250 bridge E of Fitchville, access river right	A–B	3.5	3
B. Prospect Rd. bridge N of Fitchville, access river left	B–C	3	3
C. Cook Rd. bridge SW of West Clarksfield, access river left	C–D	8	7
D. Auster Rd. bridge S of Wakeman, access river left	D–E	14	9.5
E. Firelands Community Park in Birmingham, access river left	E–F	7.5	6.5

BLACK RIVER

Although the 470 square miles of the Black River drainage basin encompass parts of Huron, Ashland, Medina, and Cuyahoga counties, the paddleable portions of the river lie entirely within Lorain County. Both the East and West branches of the Black offer pleasant Class I paddling under a leaf-canopied corridor through the woodlots and fields of the county's rolling hills.

Paddlers can begin on the West Branch at Hughes Road east of OH 58, where the 20-foot-wide channel is willow-lined and winding. This branch increases to about 30 feet in width by the time it reaches the third bridge down, at Parsons Road. Low-hanging tree limbs and a few deadfalls create the only obstacles to your progress.

Alternatively, paddlers can sample the slightly more interesting East Branch beginning at OH 303. Although this section of the East Branch sets out through farmland that is somewhat more exposed as a result of banks that are sparsely vegetated in places, by the time it reaches Grafton the banks are wooded and the stream's current has uncovered bedrock (with cuts that create a few small chutes and Class I+ riffles at certain water levels). As you near Laporte, willows take over the low mud banks, occasionally parting to reveal fields, horses, and a broad, flat floodplain.

The pastoral character of both the East and West branches changes abruptly as they enter Elyria and prepare to expend all their gradient in separate grand leaps. First homes, and then industry and floodwalls, line the banks of each branch. Then, about 0.25 mile before the confluence, both branches plunge abruptly over unrunnable 30–35-foot waterfalls into deep, rocky, moss-splotched gorges that merge into Elyria's Cascade Park. There is no place to get out immediately above either of the falls. If you wait until you hear the roar, then you have waited too long (and you had better have one powerful back ferry). The more practical alternative is to make sure you exit the West Branch at the Third Street bridge or the East Branch at the Fuller Road bridge. If you intend to paddle more of the

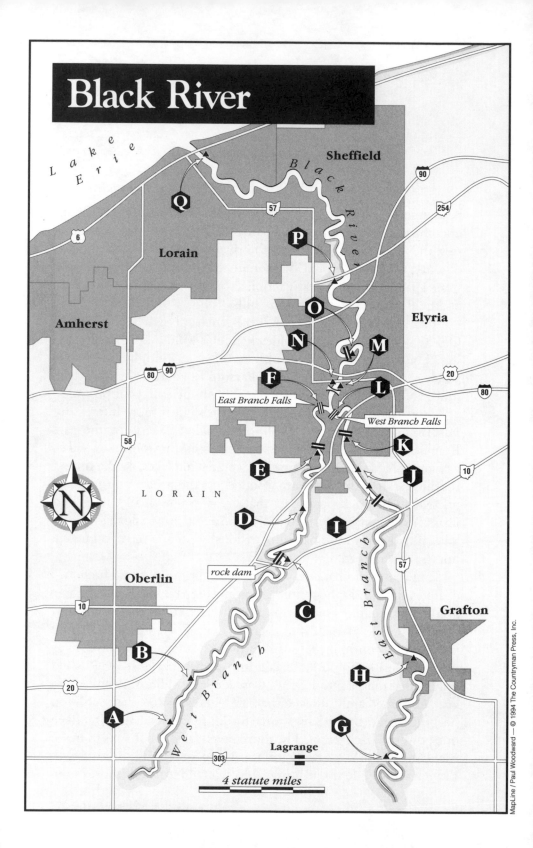

Black River

Lake Erie

Sheffield

90

57

254

6

Lorain

P

Amherst

Elyria

O

N

M

80 90

20

F

80

East Branch Falls

West Branch Falls

L

K

E

10

N

J

D

I

57

rock dam

Grafton

Oberlin

C

10

B

H

G

20

West Branch

East Branch

Lagrange

303

4 statute miles

MapLine / Paul Woodward — © 1994 The Countryman Press, Inc.

river, you will need a shuttle vehicle to get from either take-out down to the next access point in Cascade Park.

Water quality deteriorates below Cascade Park as a result of the impact of Elyria. Nonetheless, this stretch of river has a seasonal steelhead run to its credit (although we suggest you practice catch and release).

Once in the park the river discloses the reason for its name. The gorge walls are composed of high, black-rock cliffs which, interspersed with pine-covered slopes, escort the Black River for most of the rest of its journey to Lake Erie. The Black flows peacefully through this valley, having expended most of its energy making the entrance to Cascade Park. The only two interruptions in the river's gentle path are artificial ones: a ford near the downstream boundary of the park and a broken dam another 1.5 miles downstream. The ford itself is a mandatory portage; but if there is enough water, the river downstream will set up in a series of Class I+ rollers—not as exciting as the falls, but then there is a limit to how excited most of us want to get.

Black River

Counties: Lorain

USGS Quads: LaGrange, Wellington, Grafton, Oberlin, Avon

Difficulty: International Class I

Hazards/Portages: Several low-head dams, falls on both East and West branches in Elyria

Game-fish Species: Despite water quality that is considerably less than pristine, steelhead run up as far as Cascade Park in season

Additional Info: River Forecast Center (513) 421-3670, daily readings not available

Access Point	Section	River Miles	Shuttle Miles
WEST BRANCH			
A. Hughes Rd. bridge SE of Oberlin, roadside access river right	A–B	1	1
B. West Rd. bridge and Kipton Nickle Plate Rd. SE of Oberlin, roadside access river left	B–C	7	6

C. OH 10 bridge SW of Elyria, roadside
   access river right

D. Dam above the US 20 bridge S of Elyria,
   portage river right

E. Dam at trailer court at Oberlin Rd. in Elyria
   below the railroad tracks, difficult portage river left

F. Falls under Lake St. bridge in Elyria. **Mandatory take-out by 3rd St.**	C–F	5	6

EAST BRANCH

G. OH 303 bridge E of Lagrange, roadside access river right	G–H	5	4
H. Parsons Rd. in Grafton, roadside access river right	H–I	6	6

I. Dam in residential area at Chestnut Ridge
   and East River roads, portage river right

J. Fuller Rd. bridge. **Mandatory take-out before falls, river right.**	H–J	6.5	6.5

K. Dam above East Bridge St., no portage

L. Falls downstream of Washington St.
   bridge, no portage

MAIN STEM

M. Ford at Cascade/Elywood Park,
   access below dam

N. Elywood Park off Washington St.,
   access river right

O. Broken dam about 1.5 mi. below Cascade/
   Elywood Park by the golf course, portage
   river left

P. Black River Reservation off Ford Rd. W of Sheffield	M, N–P	6	6
Q. Lakeside Launch and Mooring on Lake Erie off Lakeside St., Lorain, just E of the mouth of the Black River	P–Q	10	7

ROCKY RIVER

Like many other rivers in northeastern Ohio, the Rocky River begins its voyage to Lake Erie as a small, shallow woodland stream. Although the upper sections of this river offer only seasonal paddling, under good water conditions a paddler can start as far upstream as the Millstream Pools on the East Branch. (The West Branch, even under ideal conditions, does not generally contain enough water for a comfortable float.)

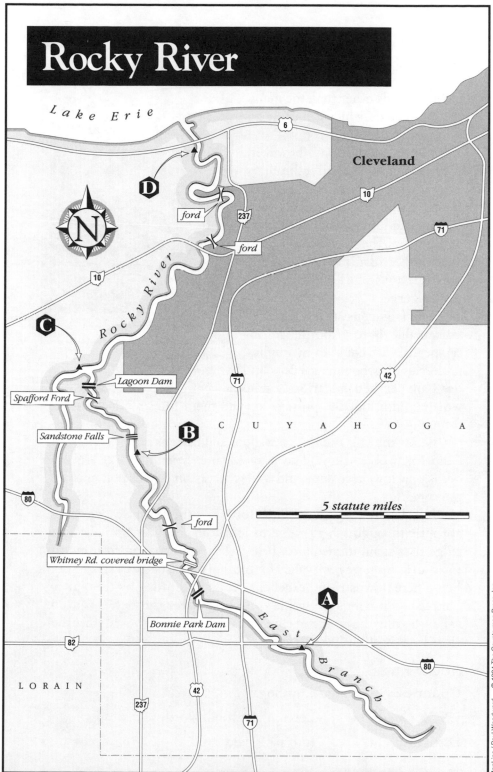

Rocky River

Lake Erie

Cleveland

C U Y A H O G A

L O R A I N

ford

ford

Lagoon Dam

Spafford Ford

Sandstone Falls

ford

Whitney Rd. covered bridge

Bonnie Park Dam

Rocky River

East Branch

5 statute miles

From the Millstream Pools down to Bagley Road, the East Branch flows gently with no appreciable hazards other than the many low-head dams, which can easily be portaged.

Below Bagley Road, however, the river begins to exhibit the characteristics that gave it its well-deserved name. Dropping between rocky banks dotted with hardwoods and conifers, the river slips over a 2-foot low-head dam just before plunging over Sandstone Falls into a rock-walled gorge.

The falls consist of a series of unrunnable 4- to 6-foot ledges interspersed with complex hydraulics, undercut rocks, boulder gardens, and

A river view through the Cleveland Metroparks system, an emerald necklace of greenspace and watercourses that surrounds the city.

deadfalls perched precariously at just about neck level. The falls are worth seeing, but the portage around them rates a Class VI for difficulty.

Below the falls the river broadens and flattens out as it enters a deep hardwood valley. The only hazards from here on are the occasional low-head dams and the less occasional fords that must be portaged.

It is shortly after one of these fords that the West Branch slices abruptly through a high ridge to join with the East Branch. The ridge rises again immediately below the confluence on river left to form an impressive rock valley for most of the distance to Lake Erie. From here downstream, excellent access is afforded by the Valley Parkway as it winds alongside the Rocky River through this deep valley, leaving the river and climbing out of the valley just before the river loses itself in Lake Erie.

Rocky River

Counties:	Cuyahoga
USGS Quads:	Berea, Lakewood, North Olmstead
Difficulty:	International Class I

Hazards/Portages:	Sandstone Falls, low-head dams
Game-fish Species:	Largemouth and smallmouth bass (there is a smallmouth run in the spring);
	seasonal steelhead run; stocked trout near the OH 82 crossing
Additional Info:	River Forecast Center (513) 421-3670, daily readings not available

Access Point	Section	River Miles	Shuttle Miles
A. Rocky River Reservation South	A–B	7	8
B. Rocky River Reservation Central. **Mandatory take-out before falls.**	B–C	4	4
C. Rocky River Reservation North	C–D	10	7
D. Rocky River Reservation North			

CUYAHOGA RIVER

Mention the Cuyahoga River to people who have never paddled it, and you are likely to get incredulous looks and bad jokes about fireproof boats and paddles. This unfortunate state of affairs stems from an incident in the late 1960s when a petroleum spill occurred in the lower section of the river where commercial traffic was heavy. The spill resulted in the river's "catching fire," which gave the media all the material it needed to depict the Cuyahoga as a heavily polluted blemish on the northeastern Ohio landscape. Water quality has improved since then, but the media attention hasn't. As recently as 1992 the *Wall Street Journal* reported a professional "Bigfoot" tracker's claims that a number of the creatures lived near Cleveland. One was reportedly seen wading in the Upper Cuyahoga near Mantua.

Granted, the lower river from OH 17 to Lake Erie is a relatively uninteresting stretch, heavy in the commercial effluent generated by the rust-belt industry and seriously polluted as a result. But apart from burning wate4rs and Bigfoot sightings, the bigger portion of this river is a relatively unspoiled Ohio waterway offering everything from a gentle float through wooded hillsides rich in wildlife to an awesome series of unnavigable drops at Cuyahoga Falls.

West Branch

An adventuresome paddler might start a trip on the West Branch as far upstream as the US 322 bridge. However, the river channel is narrow here—generally no more than 10–15 feet wide—and the terrain is marshy. While the narrow channel, surrounding marsh, and deadfalls represent minor obstacles, the most significant obstacle is posed by adjacent landowners, many of whom are waterfowl hunters and frown on paddlers who disturb the ducks, especially during hunting season.

Were it not for inhospitable landowners, the West Branch would be an ideal float for those more interested in the biological diversity of the marsh than in the rigors of white-water paddling. There are no rapids on the Class I West Branch, and the first significant obstacle is not encountered until a few yards above the Butternut Road bridge, where a 2-foot low-head dam backs up a small pond. The dam is easily portaged on either side, and the water below presents no problems other than deciding which channel to take, since the main stream divides into ever smaller conduits, narrowing to less than 5 feet in places.

Many access points from Butternut Road to the confluence with the East Branch and on to Lake Rockwell are marked with NO TRESPASSING signs posted by the city of Akron, ostensibly to protect the city from liability for injuries sustained on city-owned property. While some local paddlers report that the city of Akron has not been active in enforcing these restrictions, and some sections of the stream are served by a commercial livery, the city does have the authority to enforce its restrictions and claims to be active in doing so.

East Branch

Most of the East Branch of the Cuyahoga is too small to paddle, being little more than moist ground during periods of dry weather. Where there is enough water to paddle, the stream is choked with deadfalls and beaver dams. There is, however, a section of Class I water below OH 87 with a straight channel 20–25 feet wide and a slow, even current. There is access at the bridge on OH 168, which provides a convenient starting point for trips that continue down the Upper Cuyahoga.

Upper Cuyahoga

The Upper Cuyahoga, from the confluence of the West and East branches down its 25-mile length to Lake Rockwell, is a gently flowing stream influenced partly by the woodlands through which it flows and partly by the marsh upstream near Burton. Carrying water that is sometimes cloudy from the silt and biological by-products of the marsh, the Upper Cuyahoga courses southward, often aimlessly turning back on itself as it searches out ever lower elevations through the hills of Geauga and Portage counties. In fact, the Native Americans must have been thinking of this stretch of the river when they named it Cuyahoga, which means crooked river.

With the exception of a low-head dam at Camp Hi and one other obstacle, the only hazards on the Upper Cuyahoga are the occasional strainers inevitably present on the outside of this river's many twists and turns. However, the current is rarely more than moderate, and even a novice paddler should have little difficulty avoiding being strained. The exception to this pattern occurs where the river drops through a notch in the bedrock between the two bridges in Hiram Rapids. This uncharacteristic hazard is hardly worthy of a Class I+ rating, but there is a large submerged rock in midchannel below the chute that reportedly upends its share of inattentive paddlers.

There is one final nonnatural hazard for the inattentive paddler. The city of Akron prohibits boating on Lake Rockwell. The last chance to get off the river is the OH 303 bridge. If you miss it and the authorities catch you downstream, you will be arrested.

The Upper Cuyahoga is intimate, relatively unspoiled, and ecologically fragile. Its proximity to large metropolitan areas does nothing to enhance the Upper Cuyahoga's chances at ecological survival, although the efforts of George Hazlitt and the folks at Camp Hi Canoe Livery have helped immeasurably in preserving this portion of the river. Each and every paddler has a discernible effect on the quality of this section. So, if you're not going to carry out more than you carried in, don't go.

Middle Cuyahoga

This section of the "crooked" river suffers from a scarcity of access points, the presence of dams, and the proximity of Kent, Munroe Falls, and Cuyahoga Falls.

You can put in off Ravenna Road below the dam that holds back Lake Rockwell, although the riverbanks are steep and footing is precarious. From here the Cuyahoga courses between high, steep banks through the center of Kent. While these banks hide most evidence of the city from view, the background noise and deteriorating water quality represent ever-present reminders that you are literally only a stone's throw from urban America.

Below Kent you have the dams to contend with. All of them must be portaged. One of them, just below Kent, is difficult and dangerous to get around because the banks are steep and a railroad track affords the most reasonable pathway. Another, just before Munroe Falls, is not difficult nor dangerous, but it involves a short carry.

At this point, if you are unfamiliar with this river, it would be wise to start thinking about getting off it. As the river enters the city of Cuyahoga Falls, the banks rise on both sides—only 10 or 15 feet at first. Then there is a series of three nonnavigable dams, all of them 10–15 feet high and all of them with river-wide, uniform keepers at their bases. There is a no place to get out, and if the river is running high, a strong back-paddle won't save you. However, running these first three drops would be easy compared to what follows.

If you were careless enough to get swept over the first three dams and lucky enough to come out of the hydraulics at the base of each of them, you would then drop into the upper gorge. With sheer rock walls rising from 20 to 100 feet, recovery of lost equipment is very difficult; rescue would be virtually impossible, although the strong likelihood is that it wouldn't be necessary.

Shortly below the third dam is the first ledge. Let's call it Comin' Home, Sweet Jesus Ledge. The river drops 10–15 feet off its lip and crashes onto some very large and ominous-looking rocks—there isn't much of a cushion. The second river-wide ledge only drops you about 1½ feet, but it sets you up for the third ledge—let's call it At Home, Sweet Jesus Ledge. Most of the Cuyahoga funnels into a notch at its center and then drops 15 feet down a 60-degree water slide that narrows to 5 feet at the bottom with neck-high undercut rocks on both sides.

If you accidentally make this little journey through the upper gorge, you will cover over 0.3 mile and 75 vertical feet in just a very few minutes. And if, by some strange quirk of fate, you are still alive at the bottom, give us a call and tell us how it was. We'll write it up for the next edition.

Lower Cuyahoga

Having crashed and thundered its way to lower elevations in the upper gorge, the Lower Cuyahoga slows down behind the calming influence of the Ohio Edison Dam. Below the dam, however, is the most popular stretch of this river among experienced white-water paddlers. Access is difficult, involving a ⅛–⅜-mile portage down to the river in Gorge Park (depending on the side of the river on which you decide to put in).

Here the river drops into the lower gorge. With wooded hillsides reaching up over 100 feet on both sides, the Cuyahoga embarks on a short 1.25-mile sprint through continuous Class II and III rapids (bordering on Class IV when the river is up). The water quality here is a little better than it is above Cuyahoga Falls. The high gradient in the upper gorge aerates the river water and helps restore its depleted oxygen content, partly overcoming the effects of the high thermal load the river receives from the Ohio Edison power plant.

This environmental reprieve is short-lived, however. Soon the water added by the Little Cuyahoga (coming in from river left) and the Akron sewage treatment plant (on river right before Bath Road) convinces you that you want to avoid a bath at all costs.

You can continue your journey on the lower section of the Cuyahoga through Peninsula, but you won't want to go past the OH 17 bridge. Below that point, the by-products of our industrial society exact their by-now-obvious toll on water quality.

Cuyahoga River

Counties:	Geauga, Portage, Summit, Cuyahoga
USGS Quads:	Chardon, Burton, Mantua, Aurora, Kent, Hudson, Akron East, Akron West, Peninsula, Northfield, Shaker Heights, Cleveland South
Difficulty:	International Class I (III in Lower Gorge)

Hazards/Portages: Low-head dams, Cuyahoga Falls, difficult rapids below Ohio Edison Dam

Game-fish Species: Poor water quality in the lower reaches keeps trout from running up the Cuyahoga; the best fishing is all upstream from Kent; near the US 422 crossing, you will find largemouth and smallmouth bass and northern pike

Additional Info: Camp Hi Canoe Livery (216) 569-7621; Basecamp Outfitters (216) 657-2110

Access Point	Section	River Miles	Shuttle Miles
WEST BRANCH			
A. US 322	A–B	5	5
B. OH 87 W of Burton	B–C	4	5
EAST BRANCH			
C. OH 87 E of Burton, access river right	C–D	0.5	0.5
D. OH 168	D–E	2	4
E. Russell Park off Rapids Rd.	E–F	2	4
F. US 422 bridge	F–G	5	5
G. Camp Hi Canoe Livery off Abbott Rd.	G–H	3	3
H. Pioneer Trail Rd. bridge	H–I	2	2
I. Mantua Village Park off OH 44	I–J	1	2
J. Infirmary Rd. bridge	J–K	3	4
K. OH 303 bridge, access with permission **River is restricted from OH 303 to below Lake Rockwell.**			
L. Ravenna Rd. bridge	L–M	3	3
M. Fuller Park off Middlebury Rd.	M–N	4	5
N. Park off OH 91 (Main St.)	N–O	2	3
O. Waterworks Park **Mandatory take-out before falls.**			
P. Gorge Metro Park off Front St., access river right or left with difficult carries on both sides	P–Q	12	12
Q. Deep Lock Quarry Metro Park off Riverview Rd.	Q–R	7	12
R. OH 82 bridge	R–E	4	3
S. Confluence with Tinkers Creek			

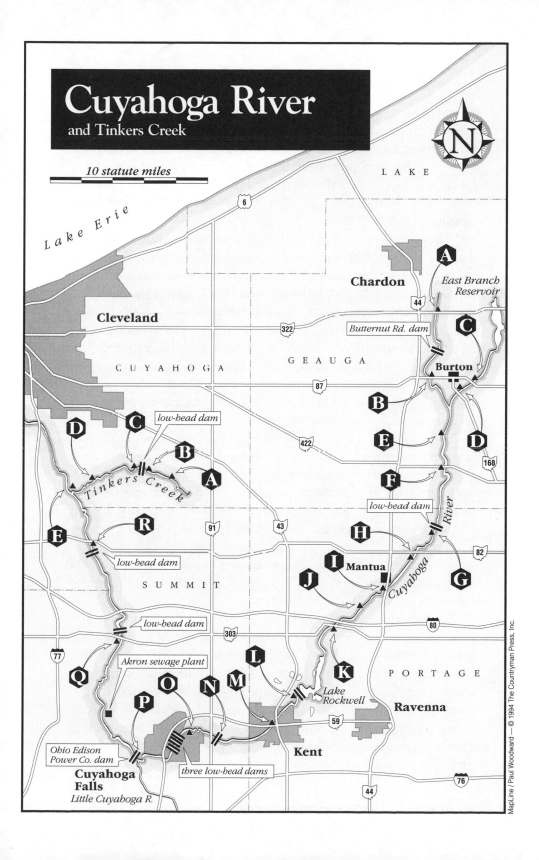

Cuyahoga River
and Tinkers Creek

10 statute miles

Lake Erie

LAKE

A

Chardon

East Branch Reservoir

44

322

Butternut Rd. dam

C

Cleveland

CUYAHOGA

GEAUGA

Burton

87

B

422

E

D

168

D

C

low-head dam

B

A

F

Tinkers Creek

low-head dam

River

E

R

91

43

H

82

low-head dam

G

SUMMIT

J

I

Mantua

Cuyahoga

low-head dam

77

303

80

Q

Akron sewage plant

P

O

N

M

L

Lake Rockwell

K

PORTAGE

Ravenna

59

Ohio Edison Power Co. dam

Cuyahoga Falls

Little Cuyahoga R.

three low-head dams

Kent

44

76

MapLine / Paul Woodward — © 1994 The Countryman Press, Inc.

TINKERS CREEK

Tinkers Creek drains a tiny basin of 96 square miles in Cuyahoga County. Consequently, it is seasonal at best and might be more appropriately characterized as a runoff stream. Nevertheless, when the water's up, this creek presents several miles of very pretty paddling from Richmond Road down to Bedford Heights and four miles of superlative white water from Bedford Heights down to the confluence with the Cuyahoga River.

The upper section of Tinkers Creek, while far less challenging than the lower section, is characterized by rocky, moss- and lichen-covered banks studded with pines and hardwoods. The stream channel is narrow and winding, and the bottom is primarily gravel and occasionally bedrock. The paddling on this stretch is Class I+, with sporadic deadfalls creating Class II surprises. The most significant hazard won't be encountered unless you miss the take-out on Solon Road. Just downstream lies a low-head dam made of jagged, boat-eating concrete usually accompanied by a collection of deadfalls and strainers. This little punctuator marks the end of the road for all but advanced paddlers in decked boats—one way or another.

Soon the creek begins to exhibit its more violent tendencies. The sides of the surrounding valley close in, and the bottom drops out as a gradient of over 53 feet per mile converts the last 4 miles of Tinkers Creek into what would appear to be some churning, primitive, Class IV ancestor of the water slide. In no time at all the stream shoots through a tunnel (runnable at certain water levels) and emerges into a narrow, steep-sided gorge. The pine-covered slopes eventually rise to 200 feet on either side, but the rock-strewn channel sets up complex currents that leave little time for sight-seeing (except, perhaps, for the underwater variety).

Hazards on the lower section of Tinkers Creek are frequent and unforgiving. The narrow gorge is conducive to river-wide logjams and strainers, and the fast current makes every paddling decision crucial. Complex currents and hydraulics coupled with limited access in the gorge make rescue difficult. Consequently, paddlers are required to notify the Metropark System before running this section of Tinkers Creek. Moreover, good sense requires a reliable roll and suggests that those unfamiliar with the stream make their first run with local paddlers who know it and are apprised of current water conditions. Fortunately, members of the Keel-Haulers, a Cleveland paddling organization, are generally available and eager to supply the requisite expertise.

Tinkers Creek

Counties:	Cuyahoga
USGS Quads:	Chagrin Falls
Difficulty:	International Class I+ (IV below Solon Road)
Hazards/Portages:	Low-head dam, strainers, difficult rapids
Game-fish Species:	Largemouth and smallmouth bass
Additional Info:	Keel-Haulers (216) 243-3667

Access Point	Section	River Miles	Shuttle Miles
A. Richmond Rd. bridge	A–B	1	2
B. Walker China off Solon Rd.	B–C	0.5	0.5
C. Metropark	C–D	3	3
D. Dunham Rd. bridge	D–E	2	1
E. Valley View Rd. bridge at Tinkers Creek Rd.			

CHAGRIN RIVER

The Chagrin River originates in the northeast corner of Portage County and drains parts of Cuyahoga, Geauga, Portage, and Lake counties on its route to Lake Erie. Although the 264 square miles of drainage, composed mainly of the East Branch, Aurora Branch, and Chagrin River, make this a relatively small system, a large part of it has been designated scenic under the Ohio Scenic Rivers Program.

The East Branch is generally considered too small to paddle, as is the Chagrin River above Chagrin Falls in Russell Township. However, below the confluence of the Aurora Branch and the Chagrin River near Chagrin Falls, paddlers will find some very pleasant, although seasonal, Class I paddling.

The river ranges from 50 to 100 feet in width through many turns over a shallow, predominantly gravel bottom. Evergreens and hardwoods do much to screen evidence of the nearby human population, and the residences most often in view are those drilled into the high mud-and-clay banks by the bank swallows.

As the river drops into Lake County, the valley begins to deepen, and the surrounding hills seem to close in, squeezing out evidence of human population and heightening the paddler's sense of isolation. When the water is up, occasional small bedrock ledges set up some Class I+ riffles. (But be prepared to wade—you know what happens when the water is low.) Hazards on the river are limited to infrequent strainers and sweepers and low-head dams at Gates Mill and Daniels Park.

Steelhead will run upstream from Lake Erie as far as the first significant low-head dam, like this one at Daniels Park on the Chagrin River.

Chagrin River

Counties:	Cuyahoga, Lake
USGS Quads:	Chagrin Falls, Mayfield Heights, Eastlake
Difficulty:	International Class I (I+)
Hazards/Portages:	Logjams, low-head dams
Game-fish Species:	Seasonal steelhead run, up to the dam at Daniels Park; spring walleye run; largemouth and smallmouth bass; trout above the dam in Gates Mill
Additional Info:	U.S. Weather Service (216) 267-5035

Access Point	Section	River Miles	Shuttle Miles
Designated scenic from confluence with Aurora Branch down to US 6 bridge.			
A. South Chagrin Reservation off Miles Rd.	A–B	7	6
B. Off Chagrin River Rd. above dam S of Gates Mill, access river left	B–C	2	1

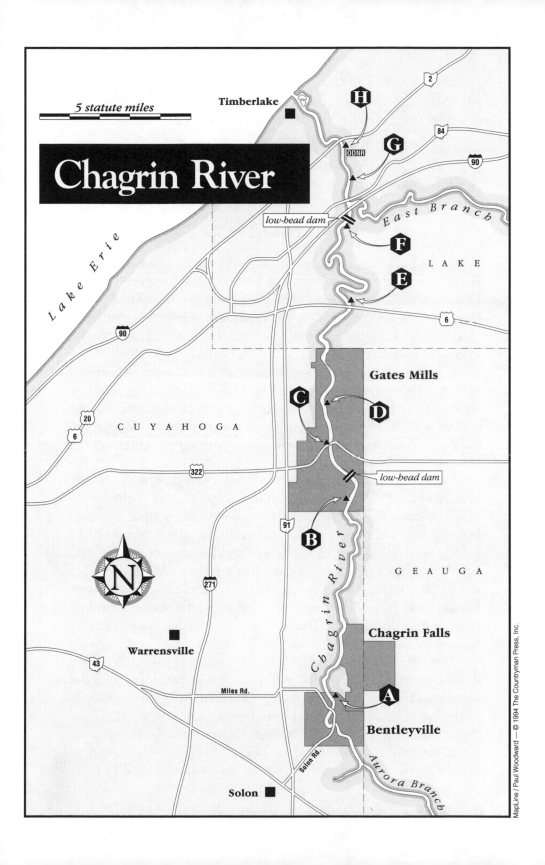

Chagrin River

5 statute miles

Timberlake

ODNR

H

G

East Branch

low-head dam

F

E

LAKE

Lake Erie

Gates Mills

C

D

CUYAHOGA

322

low-head dam

91

B

N

271

GEAUGA

Chagrin River

Warrensville

Chagrin Falls

43

Miles Rd.

A

Bentleyville

Solon Rd.

Solon

Aurora Branch

C. OH 322 bridge	C–D	1	1
D. Wilson Mills Rd. and OH 174	D–E	4	4
E. Dodd Rd. and Pleasant Valley Rd. bridge	E–F	5	4
F. Daniels Park off OH 84	F–G	2	3
G. Todd Field, off Glenn Ave.	G–H	0.5	1
H. Gibson Park, off Erie Rd./Pelton Rd.			

GRAND RIVER

Designated wild and scenic by the state of Ohio in 1974, the Grand River offers 56 miles of paddling, most of it pleasant and carefree, for Ohio paddlers of all abilities. The stretch of river designated scenic begins at the US 322 bridge, but the river is really too small and choked with deadfalls to interest any but the most dedicated bush-whacking paddlers.

It isn't until the Grand approaches US 6 that it can be paddled without a crosscut saw and an ax. From US 6 downstream, paddlers will still encounter a few logjams. However, the channel is wider and deeper here, which makes the logjams easier to get around, except during the long summer dry spells, when you may do more circum-venting than circumnavigating.

Below US 6 paddlers enter a heavily wooded valley, with covered bridges at Rock Creek and Mechanicsville among the few traces of development. This section of stream flows over a mud-and-clay bottom with little gradient, so the water is generally murky to muddy. The stream averages 200 feet in width, and cottages dot the banks, becoming more frequent as the river passes Mechanicsville.

At Harpersfield there is a six-foot low-head dam, easy to spot because it is immediately upstream from a long covered bridge. Immediately downstream from the dam and bridge is a low, river-wide ledge that sets up a small Class I+ rapids.

From the rapids at Harpersfield down to Painesville, the river is designated wild. The river accomplishes most of its descent from the plateau to the Lake Erie basin in this stretch. The river valley is deeper here; its slopes are steeper and more heavily wooded. These factors combine to keep civilization at a more respectful distance from the banks of the Grand. The availability of camping at Harpersfield, Painesville, and several Lake County Park District

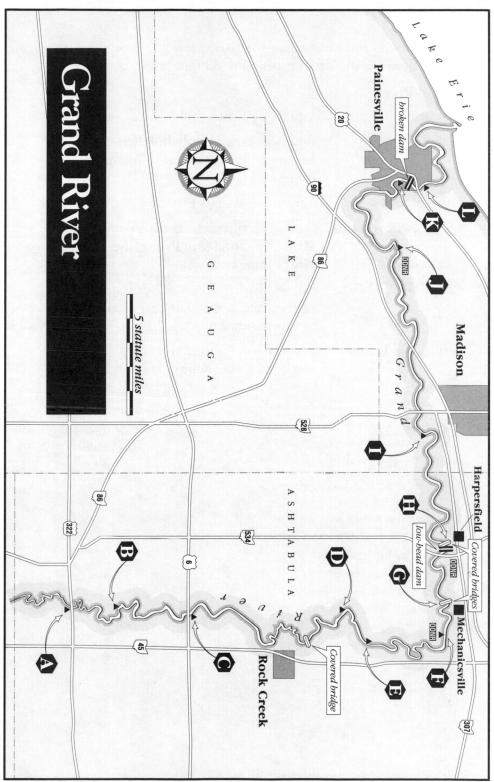

Grand River

N

5 statute miles

Lake Erie

Painesville

broken dam

Madison

L

K

J

ODNR

LAKE

90

20

86

GEAUGA

Grand

528

Harpersfield

I

H

low-head dam

Covered bridges

ODNR

322

86

B

A

45

534

6

D

G

Mechanicsville

ODNR

ASHTABULA

Rock Creek

C

River

Covered bridge

E

F

ODNR

307

MapLine / Paul Woodward — © 1994 The Countryman Press, Inc.

sites, added to the isolation of the river, make this stretch of the Grand a prime candidate for paddling/camping combinations.

Grand River

Counties:	Ashtabula, Lake
USGS Quads:	Windsor, East Trumbull, Jefferson, Ashtabula South, Geneva, Thompson, Painesville
Difficulty:	International Class I
Hazards/Portages:	Dam at Harpersfield; broken dam at East Main Street bridge in Painesville, mandatory portage river right
Game-fish Species:	Fall and early spring steelhead; spring walleye run; largemouth and smallmouth bass; occasional muskie
Additional Info:	Grand River Canoe Livery (216) 563-3486, 352-7400; Renisees Grand River Camp and Canoe (off OH 307E in Geneva)

Access Point	Section	River Miles	Shuttle Miles
A. US 322 bridge	A–B	5	6
B. Montgomery Rd. bridge, access river right	B–C	4	6
C. US 6, access but no parking	C–D	11	10
D. Grand River Canoe Livery on Fobes Rd.	D–E	2	4
E. Sweitzer Rd. bridge	E–F	7	4
F. Tote Rd., access river left	F–G	1.5	1.5
G. Windsor-Mechanicsville Rd. covered bridge, access river right	G–H	3	4
H. Harpersfield Covered Bridge Park off OH 534, access river right and left, camping nearby	H–I	6	6
I. Hidden Valley Lake Metropark off OH 528	I–J	8	9
J. Masons Landing Park off Vrooman Rd.	J–K	6	3
K. Helen Hazen Wyman Park	K–L	1	2
L. Painesville Recreation Park			

ASHTABULA RIVER

Just east of Stanhope Kelloggsville Road in Ashtabula County, the waters of several small tributaries come together to form the Ashtabula River. At this point the river is small and shallow (little more than seven feet wide in places) and flows alternately between low, grassy banks and brushy hillsides surrounded by gently rolling terrain. The Ashtabula River is, in general, a wet-weather stream; however, it takes considerable wet weather to make this uppermost section of the river paddleable.

As the river passes under a covered bridge west of Gageville and works its way down off the plateau toward the Lake Erie basin, it accepts generous contributions from feeder streams. The increased water volume, plus an increase in gradient, make the Ashtabula more interesting from this point on. The grass- and brush-covered banks give way to steep pine-covered slopes and low wooded bottomlands; the mud-and-clay stream bottom begins to show signs of bedrock. Then, brushing up against the ridge that carries Township Road 20, the Ashtabula does a little topographical contorting, passing under the road and doubling back to flow within 50 yards of itself on the other side of the ridge—in the opposite direction. Paddlers on the river will doubtless be unaware of the illusion, but from the ridge top, depending on perspective, the river appears to flow either into the ridge from both sides or out of the ridge from both sides.

In any event, the paddling begins to pick up at this point. On the downstream side of the ridge, a 1-foot, river-wide ledge clearly indicates that you are

Watch out! If the view from upstream is a smooth line across the downstream horizon, the view from downstream might look like this.

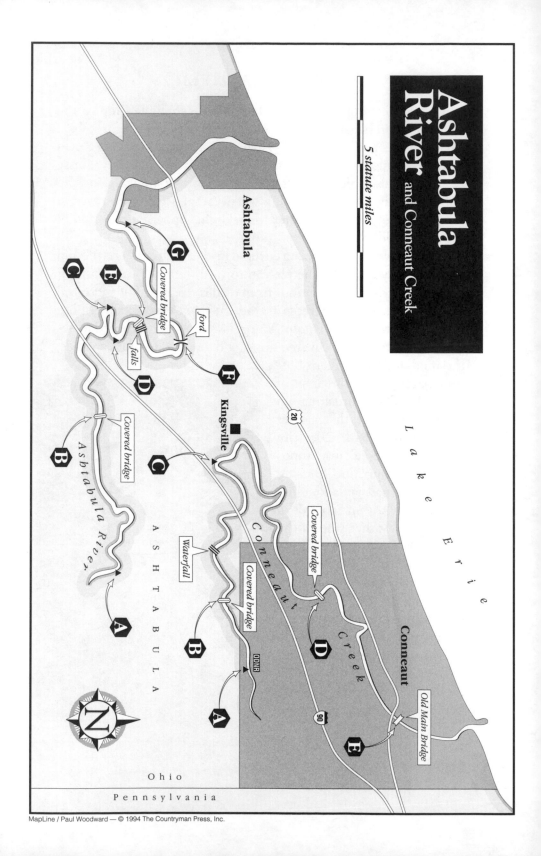

Ashtabula
River and Conneaut Creek

5 statute miles

Ashtabula

Covered bridge

ford

falls

Kingsville

Covered bridge

Ashtabula River

Covered bridge

Waterfall

ODNR

Conneaut Creek

Covered bridge

Covered bridge

Conneaut

Old Main Bridge

Lake Erie

ASHTABULA

Ohio

Pennsylvania

N

dropping over bedrock, and it marks the beginning of many more ledges in the 6–12-inch range with a few slightly bigger drops. Mix these drops with lots of water and a few strategically located bends, and you have the makings of Class II+ (III) water that can be fairly challenging for open boaters. Add scenery that is generally pretty and beautiful in spots, and you have a river that is worth paddling even under marginal water conditions. Throw in a few more covered bridges and an occasional waterfall like the 25-foot cascade just up the branch on river right below the Haddock Road ford (a 5-foot drop with some nasty concrete baffles and a mean hydraulic—in other words, a mandatory portage) and you have the Ashtabula River.

Ashtabula River

Counties:	Ashtabula
USGS Quads:	Gageville, Ashtabula South, Ashtabula North
Difficulty:	International Class II (III)
Hazards/Portages:	Haddock Road Ford
Game-fish Species:	Water quality is a problem in the lower reaches of this stream; nevertheless, there are smallmouth bass and a seasonal steelhead run for those who wish to practice catch-and-release; warm-water discharge from the CEI plant can extend your season
Additional Info:	River Forecast Center (513) 421-3670, daily readings not available

Access Point	Section	River Miles	Shuttle Miles
A. Stanhope Kelloggsville Rd. bridge	A–B	4	4
B. Benetka Rd. covered bridge, access river right	B–C	3	3
C. Township Rd. 20 bridge, access river right or left	C–D	0.5	0.5
D. Plymouth Ridge Rd. bridge, 1–2-foot ledge under bridge	D–E	0.5	1

E. Dewey Rd. covered bridge, access river left, 4-foot falls near the bridge	E–F	1	0.5
F. Haddock Rd. ford, access river left (mandatory portage)	F–G	3	4
G. Indian Trails Park off OH 46			

CONNEAUT CREEK

Tucked away in the far northeastern corner of the state lies Conneaut Creek. With a drainage basin of only 190 square miles (all but 40 of which are in Pennsylvania), the Conneaut is definitely a seasonal stream. In fact, mean flow levels in the Conneaut basin drop below 30 cubic feet per second (cfs) for two months in a typical year. However, from ice-out through May and after heavy summer rains, this stream affords very pleasant Class I+ paddling.

Like other streams along the eastern lakeshore, the Conneaut has cut deeply into the glaciated plateau in its search for lake level. This ongoing process has left the Conneaut in a narrow, sharply defined valley with sides covered alternately by hardwoods and conifers.

Beginning at the first access at Farnham Park, the Conneaut averages about 40 feet in width with many riffles and bars along its rocky gravel bottom. The gradient is relatively constant as the stream drops and turns against sharply cut shale banks, funnels between gravel bars that sometimes constrict the channel to 10–15 feet, and occasionally meanders into wide, sunny openings.

Like other streams in Ashtabula County, the Conneaut has its share of covered bridges. Short hikes up feeder streams often reveal pretty waterfalls where these tiny branches cascade down the Conneaut's surrounding slopes.

Hazards of the Conneaut are limited to infrequent strainers and sweepers, and a few standing waves when the water is high. There is one short stretch of Class I+ (II) water in the city of Conneaut around the Old Main Bridge. The channel turns sharply to the right and constricts to 10–12 feet as the current shoves its way past some old bridge piers that frequently contain a collection of logs and brush. The concrete bridge piers and tangle of logs make this a likely place to pin a boat when the water is up.

Conneaut Creek

Counties: Ashtabula

USGS Quads: Conneaut, North Kingsville

Difficulty: International Class I+ (II)

Hazards/Portages: Old Main Bridge in Conneaut, strainers

Game-fish Species: Seasonal steelhead and salmon run; spring run of smallmouth bass; year-round smallmouth, largemouth, and walleye

Additional Info: River Forecast Center (513) 421-3670, daily readings not available

Access Point	Section	River Miles	Shuttle Miles
A. Farnham Park at Horton Rd. bridge	A–B	2	3
B. Turnpike Rd. covered bridge, access river right and left	B–C	4	5
C. South Ridge Rd. bridge in Kingsville, access river left	C–D	7	5
D. Creek Rd. covered bridge in Conneaut, access river right	D–E	4	4
E. Old Main Bridge in Conneaut			

5

Streams of the Muskingum Drainage System

As the sheer size of the 8,000-square-mile basin suggests, the Muskingum drainage system offers a wide variety of paddling experiences. From the isolated charm of the Kokosing, to the short stretches of white water on the Licking, to the urban comforts available on the Black Fork of the Mohican, to the broad Walhonding, to the marshes of Killbuck Creek, to the system of locks on the commercial Muskingum, almost every kind of environment is present. If you can't find something you like here, there's a good chance it's not to be found in Ohio.

MOHICAN RIVER

Located primarily in Ohio's Glaciated Appalachian Plateau, the Mohican River drainage system contains nearly 1,000 square miles of rolling hill country. Varying in terrain and attractiveness, this system includes the picturesque and topographically isolated Clear

Streamside camping and cabins make for convenient access to the Clear Fork of the Mohican River in Mohican State Park. [ODNR photo]

Fork and the heavily traveled Black Fork, as well as the Mohican itself.

Clear Fork

Of the various tributaries of the Mohican River, the Clear Fork provides without a doubt the most eye-pleasing cruising. From the dam that backs up Pleasant Hill Reservoir and carries Township Road 3006 from one side of the Clear Fork to the other, down to the confluence with the Black Fork, this Class I stream flows through Clearfork Gorge, an impressive 150–200-foot cut into the hilly Ohio countryside. Once the hunting grounds of the Delaware Indians, this area has been dedicated by the National Park Service as a registered national natural landmark because of its virgin white pine forest and exceptional natural character.

The put-in for this section of the Clear Fork is a long, difficult carry from the parking lot at the top of the dam. Proceed, with some difficulty, about 200 yards down the steep, grassy downstream face of the dam, ending with a 20-foot scramble over the slippery rock wall to arrive, gracefully or otherwise, at the pool created by the outflow from Pleasant Hill Reservoir. From this pool, the Clear Fork drops through a Class I riffle and broadens into a shallow, gravel-bottomed stream bordered on both sides by the steep, pine-covered sides of the gorge.

The early morning sun can make paddling this section difficult, because the glare makes it nearly impossible for paddlers to see the keel-grabbing rocks and riffles that dominate at low water levels. (At least, that was this paddler's excuse.) In contrast to the eye-straining glare, however, is the soothing isolation of this less frequently paddled tributary of the Mohican, broken only by the occasional racket of a startled mallard or the dimples of feeding rainbow trout and smallmouth bass.

A short half-hour after putting in, paddlers will round a bend in the river to discover a picturesque covered bridge. Immediately below the bridge is a pool where paddlers might, on a Saturday evening, discover a youngster being baptized notwithstanding his most earnest protestations.

Below this "dunkin' hole" on river left is a state-operated campground where paddlers can spend a pleasant evening beside the waters that brought them to this part of the state. Here the complexion of Clear Fork changes. As the walls of the gorge close in, the gradient increases, the flow picks up, the gravel bottom gives way to more firmly seated stones and rocks, and shadows take over the water that was earlier bathed in sunlight. The streambed narrows in places to 20–30 feet, and the riffles become more frequent with a few of the dropping turns bordering on Class II at moderate water levels. The only obstacles paddlers will encounter on this stream are the occasional sweepers and river-wide deadfalls.

Eventually this section of the stream broadens again as the walls of the gorge taper down to the floodplain of the Mohican River, where (approximately two paddling hours from the covered bridge) the waters of the Clear Fork join the silt-laden waters of the Black Fork.

Black Fork

In marked contrast to the Clear Fork is the Black Fork (sometimes called the Muddy Fork by locals). While the Black Fork has the advantage of being paddleable year-round, it carries with it the disadvantage of being paddled year-round, by lots of folks. There are over a dozen liveries in and around Loudonville alone, and the conveniences they offer are counterbalanced by the traffic they generate.

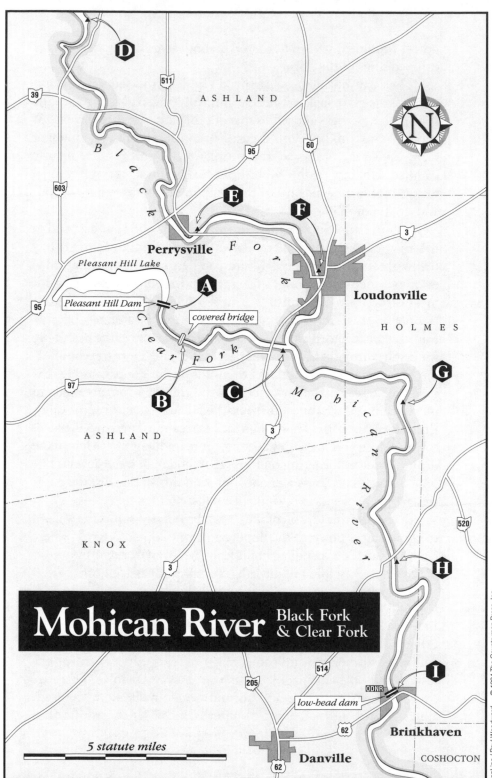

Mohican River
Black Fork & Clear Fork

ASHLAND

HOLMES

KNOX

COSHOCTON

Pleasant Hill Lake

Pleasant Hill Dam

covered bridge

Black Fork

Clear Fork

Mohican River

Perrysville

Loudonville

Danville

Brinkhaven

ODNR

low-head dam

5 statute miles

39
511
95
60
3
603
95
97
3
3
520
205
514
62
62

N

D
E
F
A
B
C
G
H
I

MapLine / Paul Woodward — © 1994 The Countryman Press, Inc.

There are many access points from Perrysville to the confluence with the Clear Fork. And while there are occasional pretty spots along this water thoroughfare, there are also many riverside campgrounds and, believe it or not, riverside carry-outs and restaurants that cater to canoe traffic. Perfect for the urban paddler, these establishments profess to offer cold beer and dry cigarettes in exchange for wet money.

Main Branch

The first 10 miles of the main branch of the Mohican are under constant recreational use. Ten miles, it seems, is the distance it takes to thin the crowds that paddle down from Loudonville.

From OH 514 to the confluence with the Kokosing, the river assumes a more isolated and more scenic character. This section of the river offers year-round Class I paddling through a broad, wooded valley down to the low-water dam at Brinkhaven, a mandatory portage despite the apparently runnable chute in the middle— the concrete baffles under the chute can be very upsetting.

From Brinkhaven downstream, the river runs alternately through grassy riffles and deep pools. Soon the river deepens, the channel broadens, the floodplain becomes more cultivated, and the Kokosing joins to mark the beginning of the Walhonding.

Mohican River

Counties:	Ashland, Richland, Holmes, Knox, Coshocton
USGS Quads:	Jelloway, Perrysville, Loudonville, Greer, Brinkhaven, Walhonding
Difficulty:	International Class I (II on the Clear Fork)
Hazards/Portages:	Low-water dam at Brinkhaven
Game-fish Species:	Smallmouth bass and stocked rainbow trout on the Clear Fork
Additional Info:	Mohican Canoe Livery 1-800-MO-CANOE; Lake Fork Canoe Livery 1-800-32-CANOE; Mohican State Park 1-800-442-2663 (see Appendix B for additional liveries)

Access Point	Section	River Miles	Shuttle Miles
CLEAR FORK			
A. Township Rd. 3006 at Pleasant Hill Dam	A–B	1	2
B. Covered bridge in Mohican State Park off OH 97	B–C	3	3
C. State park canoe Livery off OH 3/97 Black Fork			
D. Charles Mill Lake Recreation Area at the tailwaters off OH 603	D–E	9	9
E. Several liveries have access off OH 39 in Perrysville	E–F	4	4
F. Riverside Park in Loudonville and many private liveries	F–G	8	7
MAIN STEM			
G. Township Rd. 262	G–H	6	6
H. Mohican State Park Greer Landing off OH 514 and County Rd. 77	H–I	6	6
I. Hunter Road, access river left GG. (See Kokosing River)	I–GG	11	13

KOKOSING RIVER

Draining parts of Morrow, Knox, and Coshocton counties, the Kokosing River develops in a fashion that contrasts with the general pattern. Rather than rushing out of the hills to collect in broad valleys below, the Kokosing originates in the broad, flat farmland and pastureland of the Till Plains in eastern Morrow County. Flowing gently over a sand-and-gravel bottom between brush- and willow-covered banks 15–20 feet apart at Fredericktown, this seldom-paddleable section grows in size until it becomes seasonally paddleable just above Mt. Vernon. There the stream splits around a small island, grows to 30–35 feet in width, and drops through a Class I+ riffle as it begins to enter the more rugged glaciated plateau.

The river remains seasonal as it passes Gambier, growing to 40–50 feet in width and dropping more rapidly around gravel bars and through turns that sometimes constrict to 10 feet. Beyond Gambier, the Kokosing's flow becomes more reliable as the surrounding countryside becomes more rugged and more beautiful. Coursing through high, wooded banks as it approaches Millwood, the river

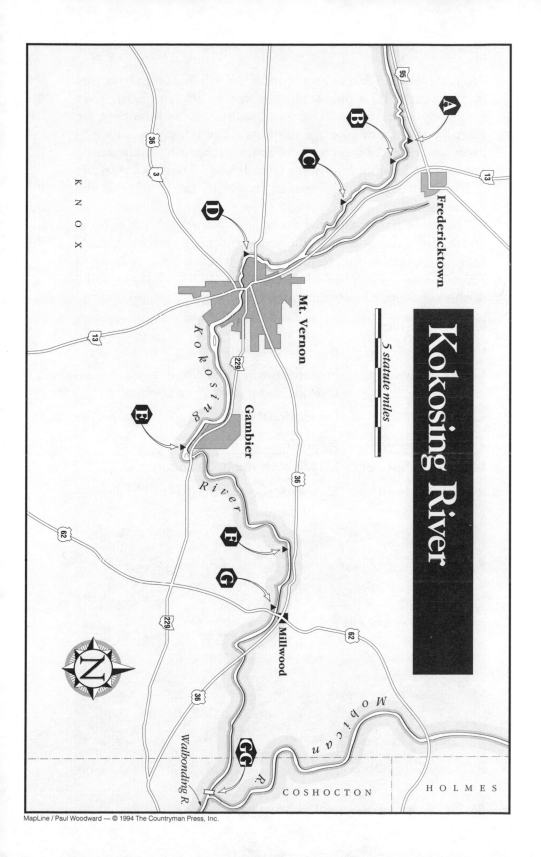

Kokosing River

5 statute miles

KNOX

Fredericktown

Mt. Vernon

Gambier

Kokosing River

Millwood

Mohican

Walhonding R.

COSHOCTON

HOLMES

95

13

36

3

13

229

36

62

229

36

62

A

B

C

D

E

F

G

GG

N

drops through a Class I+ rapids under the US 62 bridge before its clear waters enter a pine-studded gorge. In the gorge, the river frequently splits around large, flat midstream rocks perfect for relaxing on a sunny summer afternoon. The relaxation is temporarily interrupted, however, as once back on the river, paddlers soon encounter a 1½-foot drop over a Class II ledge. High rock cliffs just downstream enhance the rugged beauty of this section of the Kokosing.

Soon the river establishes a pattern. Alternating between pools and dropping turns over a mostly gravel bottom, the Kokosing winds around one final logjam before its steep, wooded banks open up to reveal a broad floodplain where its waters join with those of the Mohican to form the Walhonding.

Kokosing River

Counties: Knox, Coshocton

USGS Quads: Fredericktown, Mt. Vernon, Hunt, Danville, Brinkhaven, Walhonding

Difficulty: International Class I (II)

Hazards/Portages: Strainers

Game-fish Species: Largemouth and smallmouth bass

Additional Info: Howard Canoe Livery (614) 599-7056

Access Point	Section	River Miles	Shuttle Miles
A. Township Rd. 365 bridge	A–B	1	1
B. County Rd. 11 bridge	B–C	2	2
C. Township Rd. 401 bridge	C–D	3.5	3.5
D. Riverside Park off OH 229 in Mt. Vernon, access river left	D–E	8	7
E. Laymon Rd. bridge	E–F	6	7
F. Howard Canoe Livery	F–G	2	2
G. Millwood Rd. bridge, gorge and Class I (II) rapids below	G–GG	8	8
GG. Township Rd. 366/423 bridge at confluence with the Mohican and Walhonding, access river right and left			

WALHONDING RIVER

Lying entirely within the boundaries of Coshocton County, the Walhonding River serves as the connector between the confluence of the Kokosing and the Mohican to the west and the Muskingum to the east. The Walhonding flows a short 24 miles through a broad, cultivated floodplain with the hills of the glaciated plateau rising abruptly in the distance to either side.

Dropping at an even, gentle 3.4 feet per mile, the Walhonding provides pleasant year-round canoeing for paddlers of all abilities. The river averages 80–90 feet in width and consequently collects few snags and deadfalls; those it does collect are easily circumnavigated. The only significant hazards on the Walhonding are the Mohawk Dry Dam and the Six Mile Dam, both mandatory portages.

Walhonding River

Counties:	Coshocton
USGS Quads:	Walhonding, Warsaw, Randle, Coshocton
Difficulty:	International Class I
Hazards/Portages:	Mohawk Dry Dam, Six Mile Dam
Game-fish Species:	Largemouth and smallmouth bass
Additional Info:	Three Rivers Canoe Livery (614) 622-4080; Whispering Falls Campground (Warsaw); Corps of Engineers (304) 529-5604, daily readings not available

Access Point	Section	River Miles	Shuttle Miles
GG. Confluence with Mohicn and Kokosing at Township Rd. 366/423 bridge, access river right and left	GG–A	5	4
A. OH 715 bridge W of Mohawk Dry Dam, access river right	A–B	8	8
B. Whispering Falls Campground at Six Mile Dam downstream of OH 60 bridge, access river left with permission and fee	B–C	6	6
C. Coshocton Lake Park off OH 83			

A timely low brace (by the stern paddler) steadies these Ohio paddlers through some rough water.

KILLBUCK CREEK

Paddleable from the northern edge of Holmes County down through Coshocton County to its confluence with the Walhonding, Killbuck Creek flows through the heart of Ohio's Amish country. Paddling this stream may well take you back in time, figuratively speaking. You are quite likely to see a horse and buggy—still the primary means of transportation of the Amish—crossing any bridge over this creek.

Certainly the presence of the Amish adds a distinct flavor to trips down Killbuck Creek, but this stream is not without plenty of character of its own. Flowing through the Glaciated Appalachian Plateau, the Killbuck meanders over ancient valleys filled with a glacial till that claims poor drainage as one of its primary character-istics. Consequently, Killbuck Creek is surrounded by sparsely settled marshland rich in plant life and wildlife.

Unfortunately, the stream has been channelized in places where its unreliable drainage threatens nearby roads and villages. These relatively uninteresting sections do, however, serve to heighten the paddler's appreciation of the more remote stretches of this wood-land stream.

Killbuck Creek offers seasonal paddling for all abilities. There are no significant hazards. Inconveniences are limited to logjams and

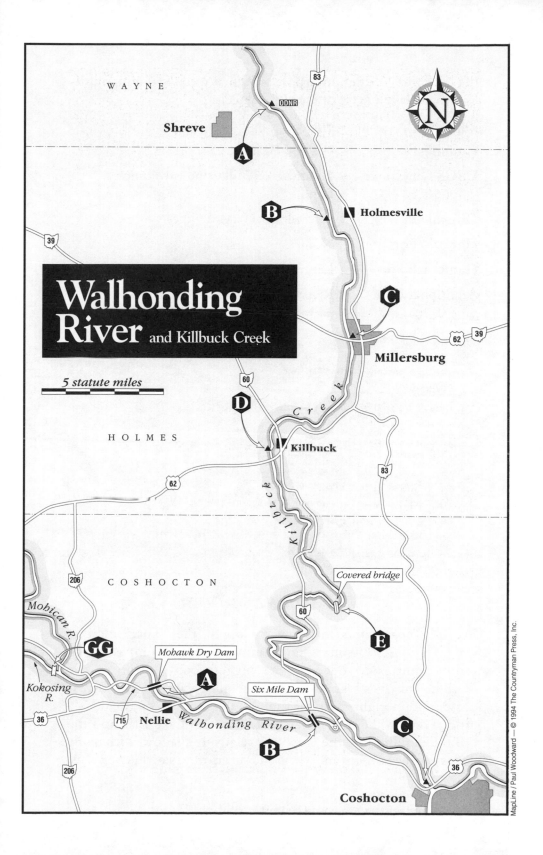

Walhonding River and Killbuck Creek

5 statute miles

WAYNE

Shreve

ODNR

A

B

Holmesville

C

Millersburg

60

D

HOLMES

Killbuck

62

Killbuck Creek

83

COSHOCTON

Covered bridge

E

60

Mohican R.

GG

Mohawk Dry Dam

A

Kokosing R.

Nellie

715

Walhonding River

Six Mile Dam

B

C

36

206

Coshocton

36

206

MapLine / Paul Woodward — © 1994 The Countryman Press, Inc.

the not entirely undesirable possibility that you might temporarily lose yourself in a maze of marshy channels.

Killbuck Creek

Counties:	Wayne, Holmes, Coshocton
USGS Quads:	Holmesville, Millersburg, Killbuck, Randle
Difficulty:	International Class I
Hazards/Portages:	None
Game-fish Species:	Largemouth and smallmouth bass
Additional Info:	River Forecast Center (513) 684-2371, daily readings not available

Access Point	Section	River Miles	Shuttle Miles
A. Township Rd. 76 in Killbuck Marsh Wildlife Area	A–B	6	8
B. County Rd. 320 bridge W of Holmesville, access river left	B–C	6	6
C. Holmes County Fairgrounds in Millersburg off OH 39/60 bridge, access river right	C–D	7	7
D. Front St. bridge in Killbuck, access river left	D–E	9	9
E. Closed covered bridge off County Rd. 343, access river left	E–B	16	15
B. On the Walhonding River			

TUSCARAWAS RIVER

From its headwaters in Summit County, the "Tusc" collects water from a 2,590-square-mile drainage basin encompassing 10 Ohio counties to become the biggest contributor to the Muskingum river system. Its size, coupled with the fact that it passes within eight miles of the Cuyahoga at Akron, made it a crucial link in the first water route between Lake Erie and the Ohio River. Because the Tusc was relatively shallow, with many riffles and snags, this route was used primarily by Native Americans, trappers, and flatboat traders, although on at least two occasions in the 1800s steamboat captains made it as far upstream as the mouth of the Tusc at Coshocton.

Nowadays the Tusc provides seasonal Class I paddling from Canal Fulton to near the Tuscarawas County line and year-round canoeing from there to Coshocton. The river flows around a proliferation of islands (some of them large) between low, tree-lined mud banks ranging from 30–40 feet apart at Canal Fulton, to 60–70 feet apart at New Philadelphia, to 90–100 feet apart at Coshocton. The Tusc is generally slow-moving and well be-haved (although there are places between the pools where the current picks up), and the water ranges from murky to muddy.

Hazards on this river consist of low-head dams at Zoar, Dover, and Midvale; a dry dam just above Dover; two sets of Class II rapids at Gnadenhutten and Orange; occasional snags; and frequent sweepers along the outside of river bends. The low-head dam at Zoar has been dynamited on river right and is runnable at certain water levels. However, the amount of water funneled through this chute and the submerged chunks of con-crete in the channel below make this run tricky for intermediate paddlers and out of the question for beginners. The dry dam at Dover is a mandatory portage on river right because of the uncertainty of clearance at the gates and the turbulence below the dam.

Tuscarawas River

Counties:	Stark, Tuscarawas, Coshocton
USGS Quads:	Canal Fulton, Massillon, Navarre, Bolivar, Dover, New Philadelphia, Gnadenhutten, Newcomerstown, Fresno, Coshocton
Difficulty:	International Class I
Hazards/Portages:	Low-head dams
Game-fish Species:	Water quality on the Tusc is not great, but you will find largemouth and small-mouth bass, especially in tributaries
Additional Info:	Carlisle Canoe Center (216) 339-4010

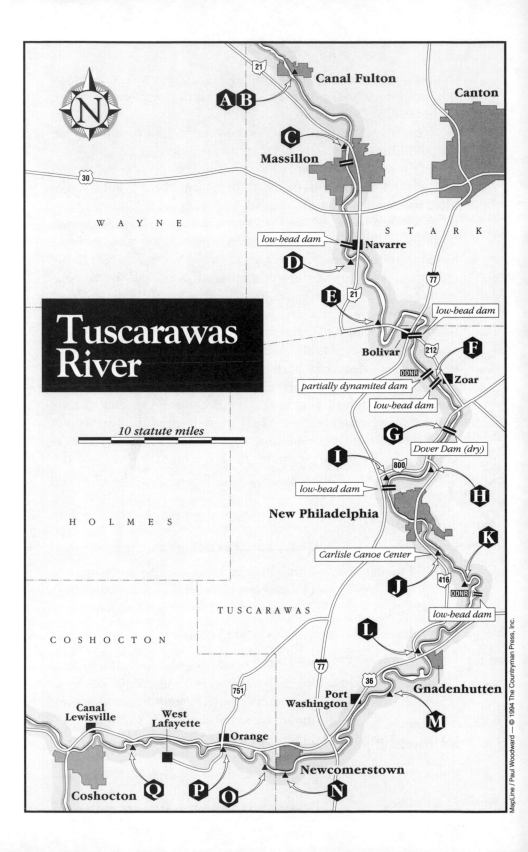

Tuscarawas River

N

10 statute miles

Canal Fulton

Canton

A B

C

Massillon

WAYNE

STARK

low-head dam

Navarre

D

E

low-head dam

Bolivar

F

Zoar

partially dynamited dam

ODNR

low-head dam

G

Dover Dam (dry)

I

low-head dam

H

K

New Philadelphia

Carlisle Canoe Center

J

ODNR

low-head dam

HOLMES

TUSCARAWAS

L

COSHOCTON

Port
Washington

Gnadenhutten

M

Canal
Lewisville

West
Lafayette

Orange

Newcomerstown

N

Coshocton

Q

P

O

Access Point	Section	River Miles	Shuttle Miles
A. Canal Fulton Park, access river right			
B. Lock #4 Park on Memorial Highway/ Erie Ave., access river left	A, B–C	9	9
C. Lake Ave. bridge in Massillon, access river left	C–D	8	8
D. OH 21 bridge in Navarre, access river left	D–E	6	6
E. OH 212 bridge, access river right	E–F	8	8
F. Closed road and bridge N of Zoar Levee Rd. bridge, access river left	F–G	5	5
G. Dover Dam, access river right. **Mandatory portage.**	G–H	2	2
H. Landing White Bridge at OH 416, OH 800, and County Rd. 85, access river left	H–I	3	3
I. Dover Landing	I–J	6	6.5
J. Carlisle Canoe Center	J–K	3	4
K. Old State Dam access Township Rd. 274 off OH 416	K–L	6	5
L. End of W. Main St. in Gnadenhutten, access river left	L–M	7	5
M. County Rd. 16 just E of Port Washington, access river left	M–N	11	9
N. River St. bridge in Newcomerstown	N–O	1	2
O. County Rd. 9 bridge W of Newcomerstown, access river right and left	O–P	4	4
P. OH 751 bridge in Orange, access river right	P–Q	6	6
Q. Off US 36, 2 mi. E of Canal Lewisville, access river right			

LICKING RIVER

Trips on the Licking River can begin on the South Fork near Hebron, on Raccoon Creek near Granville, or on the North Fork above Newark. The South Fork is probably the most attractive alternative, winding through farm country nestled in a small floodplain loosely defined by low hills to the northwest and the southeast. The only paddling difficulties on this moderately flowing fork of the Licking are the intermittent riffles, which can be a nuisance when

Many of Ohio's streams are served by liveries that offer boat and equipment rentals, shuttle service, and even advice and training. [ODNR photo]

the water is low, and the many deadfalls that often clog the 20-foot channel and can be hazardous when the water is high. Raccoon Creek is similar in nature to the South Fork, but its slightly smaller size makes it more seasonal and its close proximity to OH 16 detracts from the rural nature of the surrounding countryside. The North Fork is probably the least attractive alternative as a result of its channelized voyage through Newark.

Like the North Fork, the section of the main Licking River flowing through Newark is not particularly appealing. It flows through an uninspiring, straightened channel between uniform grass-covered levees. The only redeeming aspect of this part of the river is that it offers excellent access via Don Edwards Park. (You may want to put in downstream from the bridge there, because it has been closed to traffic and looks as though it might crumble at any moment.)

Downstream from Newark, the scenery along the river corridor improves dramatically. Shortly after the bridge on Township Road 274, the Licking starts cutting along the woodlands of the Dillon Lake Wildlife Areas. Within a few short miles the river widens to 75 feet and passes under both the old and new bridges on County Road

668. Note that the weight limits on the old bridge have been reduced—signs at both ends ironically proclaim that it is closed to ¾-ton trucks. (The bridge no longer has a road surface.)

About two miles below the bridges, the Licking enters Blackhand Gorge State Nature Preserve, one of two main attractions on the Licking River. The gorge receives its name from early Native American lore and is called Blackhand as a result of the dark sandstone formations exposed along the sides of the gorge by the river's downward erosion. Rugged topography coupled with hemlock and mountain laurel complete the effect created by the isolation of the gorge. Hazards from here to Dillon Lake are limited to deadfalls and sweepers.

If you paddle the length of 1,600-acre Dillon Lake (watch out for powerboats—there is no horsepower restriction), you can portage the dam. Less than 1 mile below the dam you will hear the muffled roar from the second main attraction on the Licking River: Dillon Falls. The falls consist of about a quarter mile of Class II rapids created by a series of irregular river-wide ledges that drop from ½ to 1 foot. At specific water levels there are some small hydraulics on this relatively long stretch of rapids, and the width of the river can make assistance from shore difficult, so you shouldn't attempt this run unless you are confident of your paddling skills. Once the excitement of Dillon Falls fades, it is a short paddle to Zanesville and the confluence with the mighty Muskingum.

Licking River

Counties:	Licking, Muskingum
USGS Quads:	Dresden, Toboso, Hanover, Newark, Granville, Zanesville West
Difficulty:	International Class I (II at Dillon Falls)
Hazards/Portages:	Strainers in Blackhand Gorge, Dillon Falls
Game-fish Species:	Largemouth bass, walleye, occasional muskie
Additional Info:	Blackhand Gorge Canoe Livery (614) 763-4000

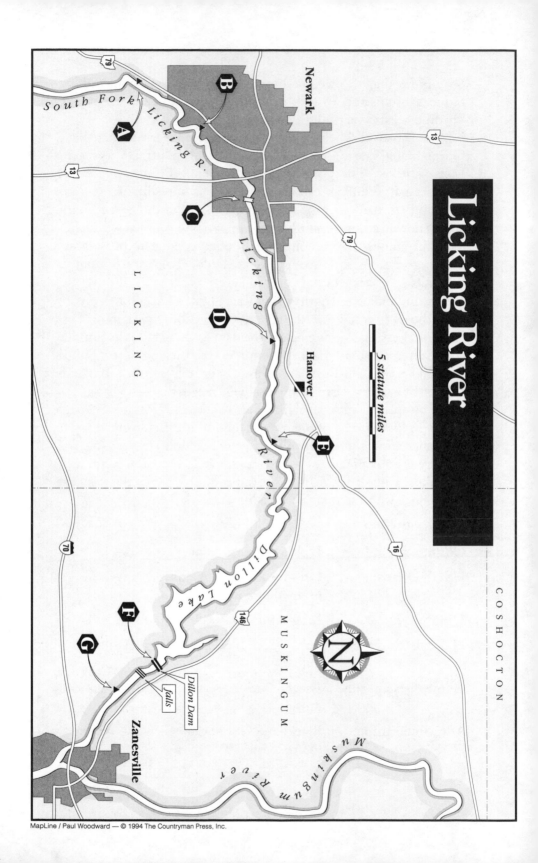

Licking River

Access Point	Section	River Miles	Shuttle Miles
A. Ridgely Tract Rd. bridge (Township Rd. 308)	A–B	4	4
B. East Irving Wick Rd.	B–C	3	3.5
C. Staddens Bridge St. bridge, Newark, access river left	C–D	6	6.5
D. County Rd. 668 bridge, access river right and left	D–E	4	4.5
E. Blackhand Gorge State Nature Preserve off Gratiot Rd. (County Rd. 278) Below Dillon Lake			
F. Dillon State Park fisherman's access off Dillon Dam Rd., access river left	F–G	2	2
G. Dillon Falls Township Park			

MUSKINGUM RIVER

The Muskingum River is the largest river lying wholly within Ohio, draining an area equal to one-fifth of the entire state. For paddlers who are in any way paranoid about the legal navigability of Ohio streams, the Muskingum is the river of choice—it has the distinction of being the only river in the state to have been formally and expressly declared navigable, by an act of Congress in 1796.

The Muskingum has its origins at the confluence of the Walhonding and Tuscarawas rivers in Coshocton. The section from Coshocton south to Dresden is the only part of the river that has never been heavily utilized by commercial traffic. Downstream from Dresden to Marietta, the 93 miles of river were opened to commercial traffic by a series of 10 dams and locks completed by the state in 1841. Traffic through these locks fluctuated until 1952, when it became virtually nonexistent and the system fell into disrepair.

In 1958 the state of Ohio rehabilitated the entire system, which has since seen use primarily by pleasure craft. The historical aspects of this series of 10 manually operated locks (early 1900s vintage), as well as the fact that they are still in operation, constitute the main attractions for paddlers on the Muskingum. The river's only hazards are posed by the wakes created by powerboats and the very dangerous keeper hydraulics at the base of each of the 10 low-head dams.

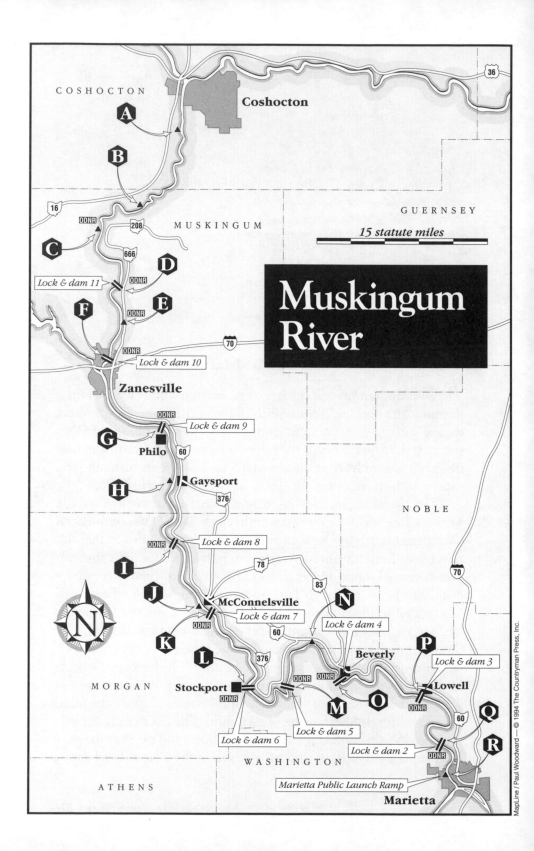

COSHOCTON

Coshocton

36

A

B

16

ODNR
208

MUSKINGUM

GUERNSEY

15 statute miles

C

666

D

Lock & dam 11

ODNR

E

F

ODNR

70

ODNR

Lock & dam 10

Zanesville

ODNR

Lock & dam 9

G

60

Philo

H

Gaysport

376

NOBLE

ODNR

Lock & dam 8

I

78

70

J

83

McConnelsville

N

Lock & dam 7

Lock & dam 4

ODNR

60

K

Beverly

P

Lock & dam 3

L

376

Stockport

ODNR

ODNR

Lowell

ODNR

M

O

60

Q

Lock & dam 6

Lock & dam 5

R

Lock & dam 2

ODNR

MORGAN

N

WASHINGTON

Marietta Public Launch Ramp

ATHENS

Marietta

Muskingum
River

MapLine / Paul Woodward — © 1994 The Countryman Press, Inc.

Muskingum River

Counties: Coshocton, Muskingum, Morgan, Washington

USGS Quads: Zanesville West, Zanesville East, Philo, Rokeby Lock, Adamsville, Conesville, Wills Creek, Coshocton, Dresden, McConnelsville, Stockport, Beverly, Lowell, Lower Salem, Marietta

Difficulty: International Class I

Hazards/Portages: Low-head dams

Game-fish Species: Largemouth bass and walleye

Additional Info: Three Rivers Canoe Livery (614) 622-4080; Mohican Canoe Livery 1-800-MO-CANOE

Access Point	Section	River Miles	Shuttle Miles
A. OH 83 bridge S of Coshocton	A–B	9	9
B. Stillwell Rd. bridge, access river right	B–C	5	4
C. Off Township Rd. 157	C–D	6	7
D. Ellis Lock #11, access river right	D–E	4	5
E. Jaycees Riverside Park, access river left	E–F	3	3
F. Lock #10, access river left	F–G	9	9
G. Philo Lock #9, access river left	G–H	5	5
H. Below bridge in Gaysport	H–I	6	6
I. Rokeby Lock #8, access river left	I–J	6	6
J. Malta Ramp, access river right	J–K	1	1
K. McConnelsville Lock #7, access river left	K–L	8	8
L. Stockport Lock #6, access river left	L–M	7	7
M. Luke Chute Lock #5, access river right	M–N	5	5
N. OH 60 roadside park	N–O	4	4
O. Beverly Lock #4, access river left	O–P	10	10
P. Lowell Lock #3, access river left	P–Q	8	7
Q. Devola Lock #2, access river left	Q–R	3	3
R. Indian Acres Park in Marietta off Linwood Ave. and OH 60, access river left			

6

Streams of the East

Few streams in this part of the state are canoeable. For the most part, they flow short distances through small watersheds with poor groundwater retention. There are several notable exceptions to this pattern, however. The Little Muskingum offers pleasant paddling through the Wayne National Forest, with a historic flavor added by several covered bridges. The Little Beaver serves up crystal-clear, quick-flowing water through exceptionally beautiful countryside. Other streams are not included here, like the Mahoning and Pymatuning Creek, but they nevertheless offer short stretches of paddleable water and a change of pace for those willing to invest some time and effort.

LITTLE BEAVER CREEK

Pick any access point on the North Fork, Middle Fork, West Fork, or the main stem of the Little Beaver Creek, and within a dozen paddle strokes it will be obvious why most of this stream has been designated wild and scenic by the Ohio Department of Natural Resources (ODNR). The rugged terrain has kept evidence of our society at a respectful distance from this gravel-bottomed, crystal-clear stream, and with the assistance of the Ohio Scenic Rivers Program, it should continue to provide sanctuary for civilization-weary paddlers. Not only was this beautiful stream the state's first wild river, but it was also the second river in Ohio to be designated scenic under the National Wild and Scenic Rivers Program.

Middle Fork

The upstream section of the Middle Fork, from Leetonia down to Beaver Creek State Park, flows through some exceptionally pretty eastern Ohio countryside, although it is only paddleable during periods of very wet weather. With the addition of water from the West Fork just above the park, the water levels get more predictable, and the stream is generally paddleable year-round from here to the Ohio River.

From the access in the center of the state park, the Middle Fork flows through a deeply incised valley. The valley's steep slopes are abundantly covered with a mixture of conifers and hardwoods, which occasionally give way to reveal large rock outcroppings and tiny, swiftly flowing feeder streams. The rock-and-gravel stream bottom keeps the water exceptionally clear and silt-free during most of the year and, coupled with the 14-feet-per-mile gradient, results in many Class I riffles. In addition to the Middle Fork's natural attractions, alert paddlers can spot the unobtrusive remnants of what at one time was the system of locks for the Sandy and Beaver Canal. Camping is permitted in the park (and is available from the park boundary to Fredricktown with permission of or by arrangement with the folks at Beaver Creek Canoe Livery).

Passing under the Sprucevale Road Bridge, paddlers leave the park, and the terrain gradually begins to change. The valley becomes a little deeper, the gradient increases, the conifers begin to surrender ground to the hardwoods, and the rocky streambed is sometimes punctuated by small boulders. Just above the OH 170 bridge at Fredricktown, paddlers will be greeted by a borderline Class II rapids that is just a little longer, a little steeper, and a little rockier than the Class I rapids that predominate upstream. If you have difficulty negotiating this rapids, then be alert, for just below the bridge is a legitimate Class II rapids that requires some river-reading skills as well as some fairly technical maneuvering. At the base of this rapids is a stream-wide ledge with a notch close to the right bank that provides the best route (the only route at lower water levels). Also, rushing in from river left, the North Fork abruptly pours over the same slab of bedrock. At high water levels these

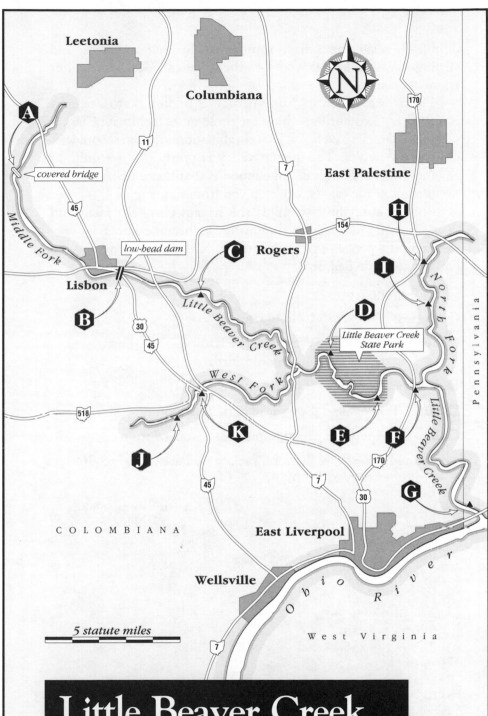

Leetonia

Columbia

A

covered bridge

45

Middle Fork

low-head dam

C Rogers

Lisbon

B

30

45

Little Beaver Creek

West Fork

518

J

K

45

N

170

East Palestine

H

I

D

Little Beaver Creek
State Park

North Fork

Little Beaver Creek

Pennsylvania

E

F

170

G

30

7

COLOMBIANA

East Liverpool

Wellsville

Ohio River

West Virginia

7

5 statute miles

Little Beaver Creek

MapLine / Paul Woodward — © 1994 The Countryman Press, Inc.

double-barreled rapids have some small hydraulics, eddies, and surfing waves, making this spot on the stream an ideal white-water training ground.

From the confluence of the North and Middle forks to Calcutta-Smith Ferry Road bridge, there are three more legitimate Class II sections characterized by various combinations of ledges, boulders, chutes, and waves. The stream valley is pretty but not quite as isolated here, although the likelihood is that the anticipation and excitement of the rapids will keep you from noticing.

Shortly after the last rapids the stream channel widens and deepens, and the gradient diminishes to become imperceptible, signaling the presence of slackwater from the Ohio River and the end of the Little Beaver.

Little Beaver Creek

Counties:	Columbiana
USGS Quads:	West Point, Elkton, Lisbon, East Liverpool North
Difficulty:	International Class I–II
Hazards/Portages:	Low-head dam in Lisbon
Game-fish Species:	Smallmouth bass, stocked trout
Additional Info:	Beaver Creek State Park (216) 385-3091; (216) 872-7755

Access Point	Section	River Miles	Shuttle Miles
A. Centennial covered bridge	A–B	5	5
B. Willow Grove Park off US 30 in Lisbon, access river right	B–C	4	4
C. Township Rd. 901 bridge	C–D	6	8
D. Bell School Rd. bridge	D–E	3	4
E. Beaver Creek State Park	E–F	2	6
F. Beaver Creek Canoe Livery	F–G	7	9
G. OH 68 bridge and Calcutta-Smith Ferry Rd. in Pennsylvania			
NORTH FORK			
H. Township Rd. 1026 bridge	H–I	2	3
I. Township Rd. 1031 bridge	I–F	3	5

WEST FORK			
J. Township Rd. 1154 bridge	J–K	1	1
K. OH 45/US 30 bridge	K–D	5	7

LITTLE MUSKINGUM RIVER

The Little Muskingum River is not at all what its name implies—it is far from a miniature version of the dammed and locked Muskingum River. Beginning as far upstream as the Ring Mill access off Low Gap Road, you can paddle this river through a small, intimate valley in the heart of the Wayne National Forest. Although the banks are low, there is little to intrude on your solitude apart from an occasional farm building, and even the nearly constant presence of the infrequently traveled OH 26 is not offensive.

The river flows gently through banks that are seldom more than 25 feet apart on its 40-mile journey to the Ohio River. There are no significant hazards; the only potential difficulty for paddlers is low water, which is frequently a problem. The unchallenging nature of this stream is not a drawback, however, because it affords time to sit back, drift along, and enjoy the incomparable scenery of eastern Washington County.

As if solitude and scenery were not enough, paddlers on this river are also treated to a little bit of history in the form of four covered bridges: Knowleton Bridge, Rinard Bridge, Hune Bridge, and Hills Bridge (camping is available at Knowleton and Hune). All four bridges are authentic anachronisms in this age of steel and concrete, and although in disrepair from years of neglect, they offer insight

Paddling the Little Muskingum, with its many covered bridges, can take you back to a time when travel was more deliberately accomplished.

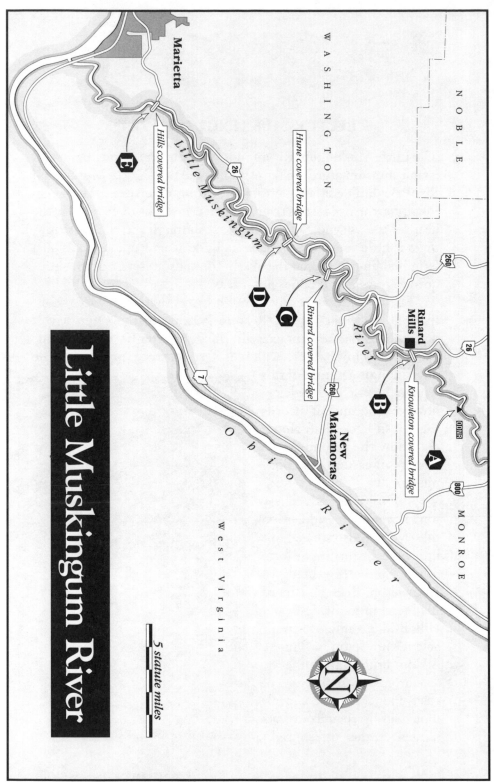

Little Muskingum River

Marietta

Hills covered bridge

E

Little Muskingum

26

Hune covered bridge

D

C

Rinard covered bridge

7

260

New Matamoras

Rinard Mills

River

26

Knowleton covered bridge

B

A

ODNR

260

800

5 statute miles

WASHINGTON

NOBLE

MONROE

Obio River

West Virginia

N

from an era in Ohio's past when getting from here to there was more deliberately accomplished.

Little Muskingum River

Counties:	Monroe, Washington
USGS Quads:	Marietta, Belmont (WV), Dalzell, Rinard Mills
Difficulty:	International Class I
Hazards/Portages:	None
Game-fish Species:	Largemouth and smallmouth bass
Additional Info:	Corps of Engineers (304) 529-5604, daily readings not available; (614) 439-4076; camping is available near the Knowleton and Hune covered bridges

Access Point	Section	River Miles	Shuttle Miles
A. Ring Mill access off Low Gap Rd. NE of Rinard Mills	A–B	6	6
B. Knowleton covered bridge	B–C	9	9
C. Rinard covered bridge on County Rd. 406	C–D	4	4
D. Hune covered bridge on Township Rd. 34	D–E	11	11
E. Hills covered bridge on County Rd. 333			

Streams of
South Central Ohio

The streams of south central Ohio are located entirely within the Unglaciated Appalachian Plateau. The surrounding countryside is, for the most part, rugged, heavily forested, and undeveloped. The development that has taken place is unfortunately concentrated in the broad stream valleys. Consequently, the larger streams with more reliable water flow, like sections of the Hocking River and lower Raccoon Creek, exhibit little of the isolation and natural beauty that surround them.

The upper sections of both the Hocking River and Raccoon Creek, however, as well as their tributaries and other smaller streams, retain the characteristics that were once common to all the streams in this area. Paddlers willing to contend with deadfalls in the narrow valleys and unreliable water conditions resulting from small drainage basins and poor groundwater retention can still enjoy a part of Ohio that has been left relatively unblemished.

HOCKING RIVER

As they approach the headwaters in Fairfield County, paddlers who drive to the Hocking River from the western part of the state will be greeted by the abruptly rising Hocking Hills. This visual teaser, coupled with the widespread reputation of the Hocking Hills as a ruggedly beautiful section of Ohio countryside, will have most right-minded paddlers eagerly anticipating their chosen put-in. Unfortunately, the Hocking has carved a broad, flat valley through the otherwise rugged hills of Fairfield, Hocking, and Athens counties, and, as a consequence, rails, roads, and development in general have followed the path of least resistance along the river. On specific stretches, the surrounding hills are far enough away that they serve only as faint reminders of the unglaciated nature of this part of the state.

The headwaters of the Hocking flow through a small hollow below Greencastle, dropping quickly over small ledges and around moss- and lichen-covered rocks. Unfortunately, the only way to appreciate the scenery here is on foot—this short stretch of river is far too small to paddle. Below this hollow the river enters the northwestern end of a broadening valley, coursing back and forth between low banks and under low bridges until it reaches 20-acre Rock Mill Lake. Downstream from the lake the Hocking parallels US 33 into Lancaster and in many respects resembles a drainage ditch.

The Hocking really does not become paddleable until after it enters Lancaster. The river also loses much of its charm and isolation at this point. Logistics have concentrated most of Fairfield County's civilization in the same broad valley that contains the river. Low, sparsely vegetated banks make it easy to see the many nearby houses and buildings, and the traffic noise from US 33 never fades for very long (the highway frequently crosses the river and is rarely more than 100 yards away). The sole hazards on this slowly flowing section of river are the frequent low bridges and boredom.

Fortunately, the Hocking becomes more palatable as it enters Hocking County. The river has by now increased to 35–40 feet in width, and the Hocking Hills have closed in, making development more difficult. The land from the county line to

Logan is primarily agricultural, and the river consequently assumes a more pastoral personality. Just a few miles inside Hocking County is a natural arch that is visible from the river opposite a small town quite appropriately named Rockbridge.

Hazards on this stretch of the Hocking include a short stretch of Class II (II+) water directly under the OH 664 bridge at Falls Mill. Just upstream of the bridge the river begins to drop over a series of irregular ledges in the bedrock, eventually lowering itself about 6 feet in the space of 150 yards. The best route is usually in midriver, but several large rocks on the lower end of the rapids require good control and maneuverability. They are not easily seen from the upper end, so the rapids should be scouted—the bridge makes it very easy to get a good look. There are no sneak routes on these rapids. (An old millrace runs downriver left, but it is not paddleable.) If surfing a hole or back ferrying through a Class III is not part of your paddling repertoire—in other words, if you are unsure of your white-water skills—the easy portage may save you an unpleasant spill and possibly a damaged boat.

The most notable hazard on this section of stream is a low-head dam in Logan. There isn't much of a drop, but the hydraulic at its base is uniform and river-wide at some water levels and has claimed a couple of lives in the past few years. Luckily, the dam is easily spotted—it is just downstream from a footbridge under which hangs a large red-and-white danger sign.

Downstream from Logan the river reassumes its pastoral character, although it never strays far from US 33. At Nelsonville there is another low-head dam; this one has a sloping downstream face that ameliorates the force of the hydraulic at its base. In Athens the river changes complexion as it widens to a shallow 100-foot channel with low, manicured grass banks. This college town presses right to the river's edge, and its presence is consequently impossible to ignore. In fact, Athens provides a good midpoint if you are planning an overnight trip but don't like the idea of sleeping under the stars. Motel signs are clearly visible from the river.

The Hocking maintains a broad, meandering character as it winds along US 50 below Athens, pulling away from the highway at Guysville but rejoining at Coolville where the even broader channel and boat launching ramp signal the impending confluence with the Ohio River and the powerboat traffic it always carries.

Hocking River

Counties:	Fairfield, Hocking, Athens
USGS Quads:	Lancaster, Rockbridge, Logan, Gore, Union Furnace, Nelsonville, Jacksonville, Athens, Stewart, Cutler, Coolville
Difficulty:	International Class I
Hazards/Portages:	Low-head dams, rapids at Falls Mill
Game-fish Species:	Largemouth bass
Additional Info:	Hocking Valley Canoe Livery (614) 385-8685, 385-2503

Access Point	Section	River Miles	Shuttle Miles
A. Mahler Park in Lancaster off OH 793	A–B	5	5
B. Horns Mill Rd. bridge at Horns Mill off US 33	B–C	6	5.5
C. Rockbridge Rd. bridge in Rockbridge	C–D	6	6
D. Hocking Valley Canoe Livery off Chieftain Dr. NW of Logan			
E. Falls, portage river right	D–G	2	2
F. Dam, **mandatory portage**			
G. Kachlemach Park off OH 93	G–H	14	14
H. OH 691/US 33 bridge in Nelsonville, roadside pull-off river left; 5 mi. downstream take left	H–I	25	18
I. Roadside rest off Township Rd. 129	I–J	14	13
J. Coolville Launch			

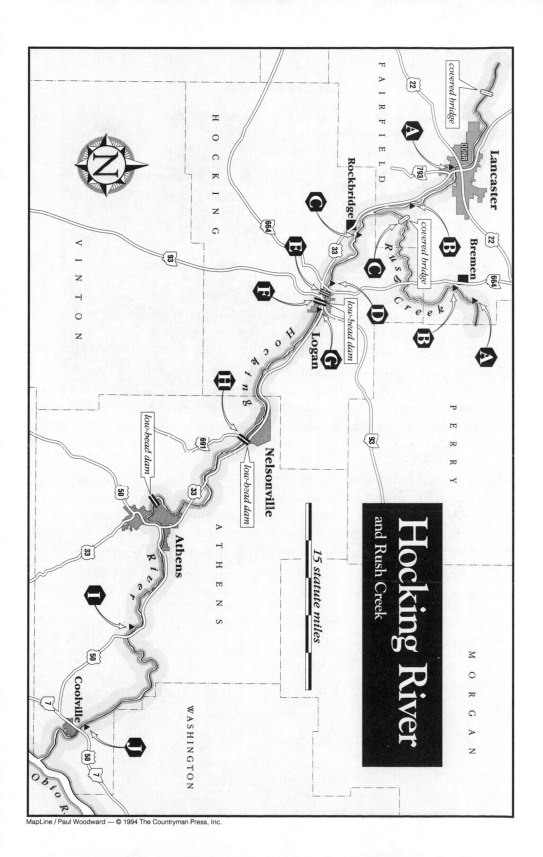

RUSH CREEK

A tributary of the Hocking, Rush Creek doesn't rush anywhere. In fact, it hardly flows at all on its leisurely 20-mile journey from just above Bremen in Fairfield County to its confluence with the Hocking River below Sugar Grove.

In contrast to the nearby Hocking, Rush Creek winds through a small valley where civilization has not displaced the deer and the muskrats and where rhododendron sometimes choke the banks, obliterating evidence of the agriculture that predominates in this valley. When there is sufficient water, this stream provides an attractive beginning to a trip down the Hocking. By starting on Rush Creek, paddlers can avoid the overdeveloped section of the Hocking River Valley in Fairfield County and join the Hocking where it is large and more scenic, without bypassing the natural arch at Rockbridge or the short stretch of rapids at Falls Mill.

Exploring Ohio's smaller streams holds a special appeal for author Gillen.

Hazards to paddlers on this creek are limited to the frequent, stream-wide logjams that must invariably be portaged. They are not dangerous, however, and usually necessitate only a very short carry.

Rush Creek

Counties:	Fairfield, Hocking
USGS Quads:	Junction City, Bremen, Lancaster, Rockbridge
Difficulty:	International Class I
Hazards/Portages:	Strainers and deadfalls
Game-fish Species:	Largemouth and smallmouth bass
Additional Info:	Hocking Valley Canoe Livery (614) 385-8685, 385-2503

Access Point	Section	River Miles	Shuttle Miles
A. Jerusalem Rd. just E of OH 37	A–B	1	3
B. Marietta Rd. just E of Bremen	B–C	13	10
C. Covered bridge on Hansley Rd. Next access at access point C on the Hocking River	C–C	11	13

RACCOON CREEK

Flowing through the rugged, unglaciated hills of southeastern Ohio, Raccoon Creek has been profoundly influenced by two factors. Immediately noticeable is the clear, green, almost luminescent quality of the water as its slips and swirls down the streambed, sculpting chutes and pockets out of the sandy bottom. This water quality is the product of local coal mining activity which, before the days of environmental awareness, polluted area waterways with acidic mine water, reducing the algae growth and other aquatic life that give most Ohio streams their murky green color during the summer months. While the water quality is improving steadily and fish can sometimes be spotted as far upstream as US 35, Raccoon Creek's water still retains its unusual translucent quality.

The other factor at work here is the ever-present evidence of a species of animal. Now you might guess that animal to be the raccoon, but if you do you are wrong. Oddly enough, the animal most clearly resident here is the beaver. There are active colonies on this stream and its tributaries, and the handiwork of these furry little buzz saws has created a maze of deadfalls and dams for paddlers to navigate. The obstacles created by these creatures add an interesting dimension to the otherwise unchallenging nature of this Class I stream.

In addition to the mischievous beavers, only the millwrights have conspired to interrupt your passage, having constructed mandatory portages in the form of milldams at Ewington, Vinton, and Northup. However, the inconvenience of lifting your boat over these low-head dams is outweighed by the flavor they add to any trip down Raccoon Creek and into the past. Rich in pioneer history, this waterway was reportedly part of Daniel Boone's trapping grounds in the early 1790s, and the relatively unblemished natural character of the terrain makes it easy for the history-conscious paddler to mentally slip into another era, exchanging Levi's and Kevlar for buckskin and birchbark.

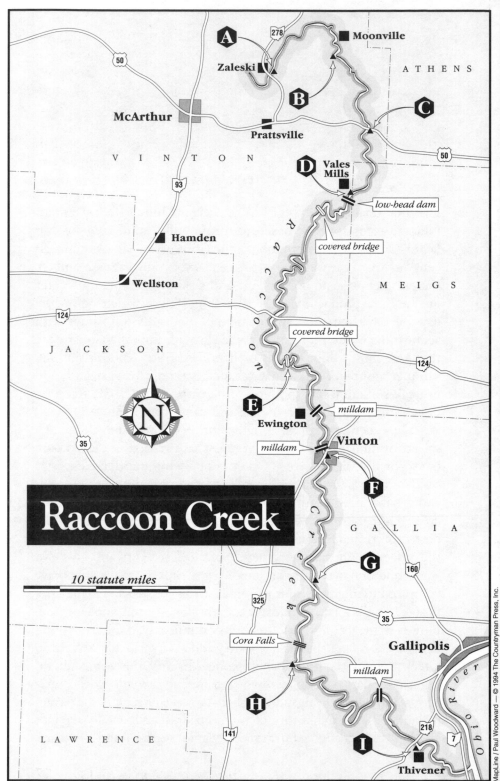

Raccoon Creek

10 statute miles

MapLine / Paul Woodward — © 1994 The Countryman Press, Inc.

Raccoon Creek is paddleable year-round from Vinton to the Ohio River. Of a more seasonal nature is the stretch of water from Lake Hope down to Vinton, as is Little Raccoon Creek, a tributary that feeds Raccoon Creek just below Vinton. However, the snags and deadfalls across these more constricted waterways may present more significant problems than low water; a trip down either of these stretches, although possible, can turn into more brush-busting than you want to attempt with a 75-pound, 17-foot handicap. In any event, the traces of history, the occasional obstacles (artificial and otherwise), and not infrequent glimpses of mink, squirrel, duck, deer, and other local residents make for truly distinctive paddling.

Raccoon Creek

Counties: Vinton, Meigs, Gallia

USGS Quads: Zaleski, Mineral, Vales Mills, Wilkesville, Mulga, Vinton

Difficulty: International Class I

Hazards/Portages: Milldams, beaver dams, and deadfalls; falls at Cora, runnable at high water levels

Game-fish Species: None

Additional Info: Bob Evans Farm Canoe Livery (614) 245-5305; camping is available near the livery and at Raccoon Creek County Park South of the OH 141 bridge

Access Point	Section	River Miles	Shuttle Miles
A. OH 278 bridge in Zaleski	A–B	6	6
B. Township Rd. bridge S of Moonville	B–C	7	7
C. US 50 bridge E of Prattsville	C–D	6	6
D. Township Rd. 31 bridge at Vales Mills	D–E	18	12
E. Covered bridge on Township Rd. 4 S of OH 124	E–F	8	7
F. OH 325/160 bridge in Vinton	F–G	10	8
G. Bob Evans Farm Canoe Livery off US 35	G–H	6	6
H. Bridge at Cora Beaver Rd. and OH 141	H–I	16	11
I. OH 218 bridge N of Thivener			

8

Streams of the Scioto Drainage System

The Scioto drainage system is the second largest drainage basin in Ohio, occupying much of the center of the state. The Scioto River bisects the basin on a north-south line as it flows out of the gently rolling Till Plains into the more rugged Glaciated Appalachian Plateau and finally through the Unglaciated Appalachian Plateau into the Ohio River at Portsmouth.

While much of the Scioto itself is not particularly interesting to paddle, its tributaries have a good deal to offer. Paddlers can sample the pristine beauty of Rocky Fork or the popular white-water run on Paint Creek. They can enjoy the lively pace of the Olentangy or the bucolic charm of Little Darby and Big Darby.

SCIOTO RIVER

The word *scioto* comes from Shawnee for "the range of the deer," and no doubt the Shawnee knew what they were talking about, for the

Scioto River Valley was one of their principal thoroughfares. However, the same topographical advantages that made this valley a likely pathway for the Shawnee also made it a likely spot for settlers to settle and farmers to farm. The unfortunate result is that the Scioto will never again be the unspoiled wilderness valley the Shawnee knew as the range of the deer.

The Scioto River empties the second largest drainage basin in the state and contains nearly 200 miles of paddleable water, but it has only been in the last 10 years that the river has become accessible. The Ohio Department of Natural Resources (ODNR) has been very active over that period in acquiring and improving river access sites throughout the state, and on the Scioto in particular the number of ODNR access points has increased tenfold.

The Scioto is a mature river with little gradient, lots of big sweeping turns, some islands, and few riffles. Without question the most interesting paddling on the Scioto is located in Delaware and Marion counties between LaRue and O'Shaughnessey Reservoir. Above LaRue logjams make the 20-foot-wide stream nearly impassable. Below LaRue the Scioto flows slowly between low, wooded banks surrounded by flat farmland and the marshes of Big Island Wildlife Area. By the time the river gets to Prospect, near the Delaware County line, it has widened to 40–50 feet, and the heavily developed banks make for relatively uninteresting scenery. Below Prospect the Scioto gets a little broader and, consequently, a little shallower. From here to O'Shaughnessey Reservoir, gravel bars, reeds, and an occasional island make for more interesting paddling, despite the fact that roads and houses are frequently visible from stream level.

Below O'Shaughnessey Reservoir there is a short stretch of paddleable water to the slackwater of Griggs Reservoir. Below Griggs Reservoir there is also a stretch of paddleable water, although the Scioto is off-limits to canoeists within the city limits of Columbus.

Below Columbus the Scioto gets much broader with the addition of water from the Olentangy River. Occasional riffles reveal that it is still a fairly shallow stream. From here to Chillicothe the Scioto flows between low, sparsely vegetated banks in an intensively farmed floodplain with no discernible boundaries. With many long, straight

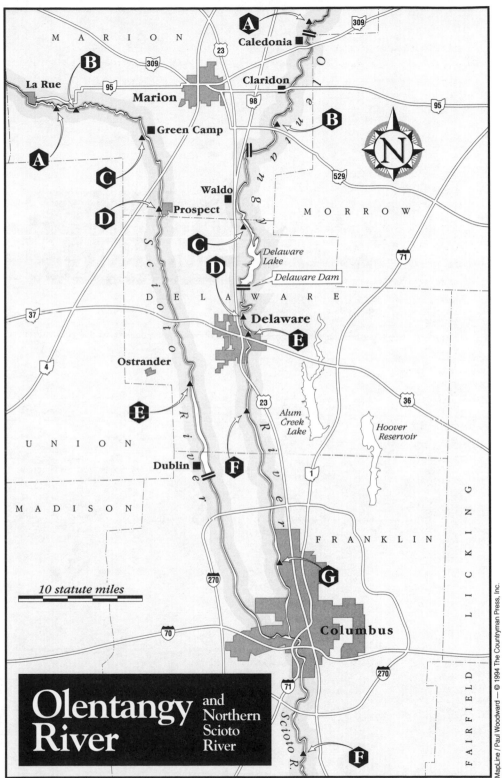

MARION

309

23

A
Caledonia

309

B

La Rue

95

Marion

Claridon

98

Green Camp

B

529

N

95

A

C

D

Waldo

Prospect

MORROW

71

C

D

Delaware
Lake

Delaware Dam

DELAWARE

37

Delaware

E

4

Ostrander

36

E

Alum
Creek
Lake

Hoover
Reservoir

UNION

23

Dublin

F

1

MADISON

FRANKLIN

LICKING

270

G

10 statute miles

70

71

Columbus

270

FAIRFIELD

Olentangy River and Northern Scioto River

71

Scioto R.

F

MapLine / Paul Woodward — © 1994 The Countryman Press, Inc.

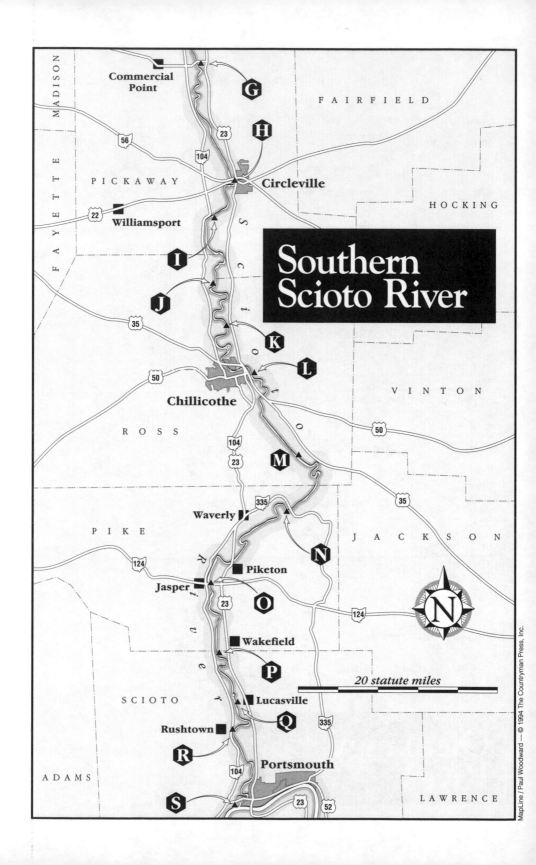

Southern Scioto River

MADISON

Commercial Point

FAIRFIELD

G

H

FAYETTE

56

104

PICKAWAY

22

Williamsport

Circleville

HOCKING

I

J

35

Scioto

K

L

VINTON

50

Chillicothe

ROSS

104

23

M

50

335

Waverly

35

PIKE

N

124

Piketon

River

Jasper

23

O

JACKSON

124

Wakefield

P

20 statute miles

SCIOTO

Lucasville

Q

335

Rushtown

R

Portsmouth

ADAMS

104

S

23

52

LAWRENCE

N

MapLine / Paul Woodward — © 1994 The Countryman Press, Inc.

stretches, this section of river simply does not have the diversity to hold even the most patient paddler's interest for very long. Even below Chillicothe, where the hills of the glaciated plateau begin to close in on the river, the floodplain is still very broad and still intensively cultivated. This pattern persists all the way to Portsmouth, where the distant, rugged hills of Shawnee State Forest are only faintly visible above the muddy banks of the Scioto. The river's silt-laden waters merge with those of the Ohio without ever revealing to paddlers much of the beauty of the surrounding countryside.

Scioto River

Counties:	Marion, Delaware, Franklin, Pickaway, Ross, Pike, Scioto
USGS Quads:	LaRue, New Bloomington, Marion West, Prospect, Ostrander, Shawnee Hills, Powell, Northwest Columbus, Southwest Columbus, Commercial Point, Darbyville, Lockbourne, Ashville, Williamsport, Martinsville, Circleville, Kingston, Andersonville, Chillicothe East, Waverly North, Richmond Dale, Waverly South, Piketon, Wakefield, West Portsmouth, New Boston, Friendship (KY)
Difficulty:	International Class I
Hazards/Portages:	Dam at Marion–Delaware county line; O'Shaughnessey Reservoir Buoys #2 and #6 to dam; Griggs Reservoir Buoy #5 to dam; dam at Dublin water treatment plant off OH 33, portage river left; canal dam about 1.25 mi. S of the OH 22 bridge in Circleville, portage river left if necessary
Game-fish Species:	Largemouth and smallmouth bass
Additional Info:	Shawnee Adventures Inc. (614) 353-8333; River Forecast Center (513) 684-2371, daily readings not available

Access Point	Section	River Miles	Shuttle Miles
A. Township Rd. 39, access river right	A–B	2.5	2.5
B. Township Rd. 35, access river right and left	B–C	6	8
C. Green Camp Park	C–D	6.5	7
D. OH 47 bridge in Prospect	D–E	16	16
E. Bellpoint Rd. bridge in Bellpoint O'Shaughnessy and Griggs reservoirs and Columbus	E–F		
F. OH 665 bridge in Shadeville	F–G	4	5
G. OH 762 bridge E of Commercial Point, access river right and left	G–H	14	13
H. US 22/OH 56 bridge in Circleville, access river right or left	H–I	6	6
I. Canal Rd.	I–J	8	8
J. Kellenberger Rd. bridge	J–K	7	7
K. Delano Rd.	K–L	9	7
L. Yoctangee Park in Chillicothe	L–M	11	12
M. Higby Rd. bridge	M–N	10	7
N. OH 335 bridge	N–O	14	13
O. OH 104 bridge in Jasper at Noname Creek, access river right	O–P	8	7
P. Camp Creek confluence with Scioto off OH 104 bridge SW of Wakefield, access river right	P–Q	6.5	6
Q. Robert-Lucas Rd./Scioto St. in Lucasville (dead-ends at river), access river left	Q–R	4.5	3
R. Scioto Brush Creek confluence off OH 104 at Rushtown	R–S	10	9
S. OH 73/104 bridge at the river mouth in Portsmouth, access river right			

PAINT CREEK

Paint Creek is navigable year-round from the Paint Creek Lake Reservoir, which is bisected by the Highland–Ross county line, and in wet weather it is navigable as far upstream as Eyman Park in Washington Courthouse. From the dam, Paint Creek flows slowly almost due south for less than 1 mile, with Highland County on the west bank and Ross County on the east. This short stretch tends to be flat, deep, and relatively uninteresting. The stream then turns due east, and shortly after Rocky Fork empties in on river right, Paint Creek drops into scenic Paint Valley in a quarter-mile run of white water known to locals as the Chutes. The Chutes approach Class III in difficulty when Paint Creek is releasing 700–1,100 cubic feet per second (cfs).

At the head of this rapids the river is wide and shallow, with some standing waves at high water levels. The stream then forks into two deep, swift channels that drop over a series of three limestone ledges with hydraulics followed by high standing waves. The left channel slopes more gradually than the right, but at minimum runnable water levels the second ledge harbors a large, submerged, and difficult-to-avoid rock.

Scouting the Chutes is warranted, particularly if you've never run them. The most commonly employed strategy is to run the first drop near the left bank, ferry across the stream, and take the second drop just to the right of a tiny island aptly named Turtle Rock. You can eddy out behind Turtle Rock or continue downstream, moving laterally to the left side of the stream and over the third drop near the

The Chutes on Paint Creek at higher water levels are a popular training run for members of the Cincinnati Sierra Club Canoe/Kayak School.

left bank. At this point most of the water in the stream funnels into one fast, deep channel with high standing waves. While the danger rapidly diminishes after the third drop, a spill at this falls can mean a fairly long swim; it's a good idea, particularly in winter and early spring when the water is frigid, to have someone waiting in an eddy downstream, prepared to make a quick rescue.

After the Chutes the stream winds placidly through beautiful Paint Valley, which extends almost the length of Ross County. With the exception of riffles and small drops here and there, the peacefulness is interrupted only once—at the falls about 2.5 miles downstream from the Chutes.

The falls of Paint Creek can be run by experienced paddlers if water levels are right. If the current is not too strong, and if you have a strong back ferry, you can approach the falls with caution, moving laterally along the stream above the falls searching for a place to drop through. At certain water levels paddlers can avail themselves of a sneak route along the right bank. In any case, the falls (Class III) are not to be taken lightly; they are (at less than optimum water conditions) deceptively tricky, with large, jagged, strategically placed rocks awaiting overconfident or inexperienced paddlers.

The western or upstream half of Paint Creek in particular is beautiful. Here Paint Valley is an almost flat plain several miles wide with steep, wooded hills on the horizon. Farther downstream the valley tends to be more populated, especially approaching Chillicothe.

Paint Creek

Counties:	Ross
USGS Quads:	Greenfield, Rainsboro, Bainbridge, South Salem, Morgantown, Bourneville, Chillicothe West, Chillicothe East
Difficulty:	International Class I+ (III)
Hazards/Portages:	Class III rapids, falls
Game-fish Species:	Saugeye, smallmouth bass
Additional Info:	Paint Creek Lake Information (24-hour recording) (513) 365-1167

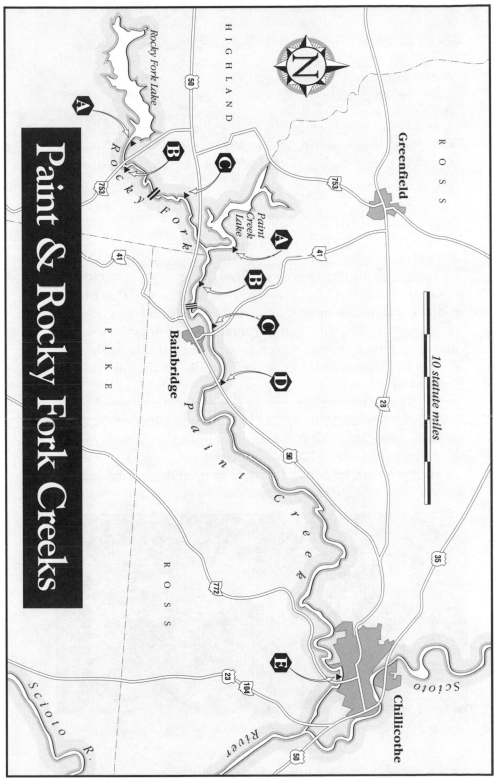

Paint & Rocky Fork Creeks

Rocky Fork Lake

HIGHLAND

Greenfield

ROSS

Paint Creek Lake

Bainbridge

PIKE

ROSS

Chillicothe

Scioto River

Scioto R.

10 statute miles

Access Point	Section	River Miles	Shuttle Miles
A. Paint Creek State Park lake below dam S of Greenfield	A–B	3.5	3
B. Roadside Rest on OH 50 W of Bainbridge	B–C	3.5	3.5
C. Quarry St. (OH 41) bridge in Bainbridge	C–D	3	3
D. OH 50 bridge, park at Seip Mound State Memorial	D–E	24	18.5
E. OH 772 bridge in Chillicothe			

ROCKY FORK CREEK

This small, boulder-strewn creek framed by rocky overhangs and stands of cedar interspersed among the sycamores and other hardwoods is easily one of the most beautiful streams in the state. Somewhat seasonal, with a quick runoff, Rocky Fork carves its way through dolomite gorges and winds through the steep hills of western Highland County before joining Paint Creek at the Ross County line.

With no industry to pollute it, Rocky Fork remains relatively unspoiled; wildlife is abundant, and fishing for smallmouth bass and saugeye is excellent, with an occasional muskie being taken, usually close to the reservoir of Rocky Fork Lake.

Rocky Fork starts slowly in its descent from Rocky Fork Lake to Paint Valley, winding through a series of long pools punctuated by

Author Combs takes a break from paddling to make a few casts in a promising pool.

shallow riffles. The gradient increases gradually, and the current quickens, with just enough tight turns and forks farther downstream to demand your attention at the right water levels. (A good rule of thumb on Rocky Fork is to take the left channel whenever the stream forks.)

About 3.5 miles downstream from the OH 753 bridge, soon after Pickett Run empties into the creek on river right, is an old milldam that must be portaged. (You'll see the washed-out remnants of the Barrett Mill Road bridge immediately below the dam.) Just downstream, after the Browning Road bridge, lies perhaps the most scenic portion of the stream. Rolling hills give way to the more rugged terrain of limestone escarpments and boulders, and at one point the stream has carved its way through two house-size boulders to form a natural bridge covered with colorful lichens and scraggly evergreens.

Local paddlers frequently put in at the Browning Road access, combining a cruise on the more scenic stretch of Rocky Fork Creek with a good Class III white-water run just below the confluence of Rocky Fork and Paint Creek.

Rocky Fork Creek

Counties:	Highland
USGS Quads:	Rainsboro, Bainbridge
Difficulty:	International Class I (II)
Hazards/Portages:	Dam, strainers
Game-fish Species:	Muskies (near lake), walleye, saugeye, smallmouth bass
Additional Info:	Huntington Corps of Engineers (304) 529-5602

Access Point	Section	River Miles	Shuttle Miles
A. Rocky Fork State Park off US 50, below dam	A–B	2	2
B. Spargur Lane Rd. OH 753 bridge	B–C	5.5	8
C. Browning Rd. bridge			

BIG DARBY CREEK

The Nature Conservancy has declared the Big Darby Creek to be one of the "Last Great Places" in the Western Hemisphere. This Nature Conservancy bioreserve supports 100 species of fish (including the endangered Scioto Madtom Darter), 40 species of freshwater mussels, 176 species of birds, 34 species of mammals, and 31 species of reptiles and amphibians—if you can't find it here, then you're just not going to find it.

The headwaters of Big Darby Creek come together in Logan County not far from the highest point in the state near Bellefontaine. From here the stream winds its way in slow, looping curves in a southeasterly direction to the Scioto near Circleville. The Big Darby flows through the dairy farms and rolling hills typical of central Ohio. The countryside tends to be open, with hardwoods spaced widely along the banks, but there are small woodlots here and there.

The Big Darby is a Class I stream suitable for novices or families and pretty enough to appeal to anyone interested in a leisurely fair-weather cruise. The current is slow to moderate, with infrequent shoals but no real white water. Strainers and logjams are seldom a problem, even on the upper stretches of the creek. The Big Darby is usually canoeable in the spring and in rainy weather in the summer.

Several miles south of US 40 is a small low-head dam that must be portaged on river right. Several miles farther downstream is another dam, followed immediately by three rock dams. To portage these, paddlers should get permission from the owners at (614) 460-4444. Or avoid the hassle by putting in downstream from the dam.

The Big Darby is designated scenic from the Champaign–Union county line downstream to the Conrail railroad trestle, and from the confluence with the Little Darby downstream to the Scioto River.

Big Darby Creek

Counties:	Union, Madison, Franklin, Pickaway
USGS Quads:	Milford Center, Marysville, Plain City, Hilliard, West Jeff Galloway, Harrisburg, Five Points, Darbyville, Circleville

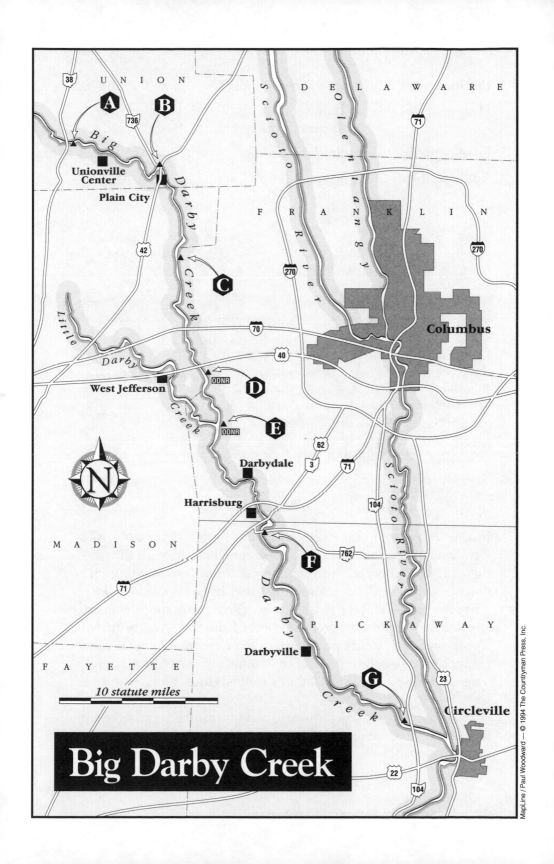

Difficulty:	International Class I
Hazards/Portages:	Dam south of US 40, occasional strainers upstream from point
Game-fish Species:	Smallmouth bass
Additional Info:	Trapper John's Canoe Livery (614) 877-4321

Access Point	Section	River Miles	Shuttle Miles
A. Burns Rd. bridge S of Marysville off OH 38	A–B	8	7
B. OH 736 and US 42 bridge	B–C	7	7
C. Smith-Calhoun Rd. and Price-Hilliards Rd. bridge	C–D	8	8
D. Riverside and Darby drives beneath US 40 bridge (beware several dams below US 40)	D–E	5	6
E. Batelle Darby Creek Park off Alkire Rd. and Gardner Rd. at mouth of Little Darby	E–F	9	7.5
F. Old Harrisburg Rd. and US 62/OH 63 bridge E of Harrisburg	F–G	20	18
G. SR 104 NW of Circleville			

OLENTANGY RIVER

From Delaware Lake to its confluence with the Scioto, the Olentangy flows quickly over a limestone bed through the rolling hills of Delaware and Franklin counties. Surroundings are typical of central Ohio, alternating between farms and woodlots. The region is densely populated, increasingly so as the Olentangy approaches the estates of the Loch Lomond area north of Columbus. Despite its proximity to the city, the Olentangy is a pretty stream—prettier in fact than some more rural waterways. The Olentangy is central Ohio's only state-designated scenic river.

The moderately quick current, rocky streambed, and frequent limestone ledges make paddling this lively Class I+ stream thoroughly enjoyable. One stretch of approximately 7 miles that flows through Stratford approaches Class III in difficulty when the river is running at 1,000 cfs or higher. The Olentangy provides good practice in sharpening beginners' navigation and river-reading skills.

There is one substantial hazard on the Olentangy in the form of numerous lowhead dams. In the stretch from Delaware Lake to a few miles south of the city of Delaware, paddlers will encounter no fewer than five dams. The second of these, in Delaware, appears washed out in the center, and many paddlers attempt to run it. Don't. A large and nearly undetectable rock immediately below the chute invariably upends those who try it.

Rocky Fork Creek, in the Seven Caves region, presents dramatic cliffs, rock ledges, and even a rock bridge for adventuresome Ohio paddlers.

A good rule of thumb when approaching the US 23 bridge south of town is to stay to the extreme right side of the river. Two shallow, river-wide shelves can usually be navigated to the right, a dam near the bridge must be portaged to the right, and another very small makeshift dam is mostly washed out and can usually be run to the right.

From the Delaware Lake down, the Olentangy is generally runnable in the spring when the dam is released. Local canoeing groups, most notably the Columbus-based AYH (see data table and Appendix C), occasionally arrange dam releases with the Huntington Corps of Engineers at Delaware Lake.

Upstream from Delaware Lake the riverbed is silted over for the most part. The upper section is scenic and less densely populated than the lower but tends to run flat, and logjams can be a problem the farther north you go. The upper Olentangy is strictly a wet-weather stream. (A map of the Olentangy River is on page 131.)

Olentangy River

Counties: Marion, Delaware, Franklin

USGS Quads: Caledonia, Denmark, Marion East, Waldo, Delaware, Powell, Northwest Columbus, Southwest Columbus

Difficulty: International Class I (III)

Hazards/Portages: Dams

Game-fish Species: Smallmouth bass

Additional Info: Delaware Reservoir (614) 363-4011; Columbus AYH (614) 891-6362

Access Point	Section	River Miles	Shuttle Miles
A. Linn-Hipsher Rd. bridge	A–B	10	9
B. OH 529/Whetstone River Rd.	B–C	11	10
C. Delaware State Park N of Delaware	C–D	8.5	7.5
D. US 23/Panhandle Rd. bridge	D–E	2	1.5
E. Mingo Park in Delaware	E–F	6.5	8.5
F. Hyatts Rd. bridge	F–G	12	11.5
G. Whetstone Park of Roses/Northstone Park between North St. and Henderson St., river left			

9

Streams of the
Southwest

Southwestern Ohio contains two drainage systems, the Great Miami River and the Little Miami River, both of which flow parallel in a southwesterly direction to the Ohio. The larger of the two is, as you might expect, the Great Miami, which begins at Indian Lake north of Bellefontaine and bisects the region on its way to the Ohio at the southwestern corner of the state.

Terrain in the region varies from generally flat in some northern and western sections, to rolling in the central parts, to steeper, wooded hillsides approaching the Ohio River Valley. Flatter regions are mainly agricultural, while the hillier river valleys alternate between agricultural bottomlands and wooded hillsides. There are a few conifers in this part of the state; timber consists primarily of older second-growth hardwoods. Sycamores and cottonwoods predominate along the stream banks.

Groundwater retention is fairly good, making for consistent flow levels in the larger streams. Only minor tributaries and the headwaters of the bigger streams are seasonal.

Water quality and scenery on the Great Miami, particularly between Dayton and Hamilton, are generally poor. Upstream from

Dayton the Great Miami affords pleasant paddling. The Little Miami and its tributaries, as well as the upper reaches of the Great Miami tributaries, also offer some attractive and worthwhile paddling.

Unfortunately, nature didn't develop Ohio's drainage systems with a canoe guidebook in mind. Several streams in Ohio don't fit neatly into any geographical categories. Among them are White Oak Creek and Ohio Brush Creek—the two navigable streams in a group of about two dozen small streams between Cincinnati and Portsmouth that flow a short distance to the Ohio River. The White Oak drains about 234 square miles of territory made up mostly of dense glacial till. Underlying bedrock, exposed in many places, is impervious shale and limestone, making for an extremely low dry-weather flow. Ohio Brush Creek flows somewhat more consistently through the rugged, unglaciated territory in Adams County and drains an area of nearly 435 square miles.

GREAT MIAMI RIVER

The Miami River Valley ranks among the most heavily industrialized areas in the nation, and the sections flowing through Dayton and Hamilton offer strictly urban paddling. Still, much progress has

Author Gillen tests a new pair of "boat shoes" on the East Fork of the Little Miami River.

been made in recent years in cleaning up the Great Miami, and the paddler who avoids the more congested areas can enjoy scenic, peaceful paddling through the rolling hills of southwestern Ohio's farm country.

The Miami was once a free-flowing river that served as a major artery in the transportation network of the Native Americans who inhabited the region, including the tribe after which the river was named. Early settlers built towns that grew into cities in the flood-plains of the river, and after the flood of 1913, the Miami Conservancy District was established to dredge, channel, dam, and levee the Miami and its tributaries into submission. Low-head dams are still a prominent feature on the Great Miami, making for slow paddling on some stretches and creating hazards at high water levels.

North of Dayton, the river retains many of its free-flowing characteristics. Much of the river between its origin at Indian Lake and the suburbs of Dayton flows through wide expanses of farm country and is bordered by cornfields and woodlots. The northern-most stretch, in Logan County, runs generally slow and straight; for the first 7 or 8 miles the river is narrow and runs between steep banks, appearing as though it has been dredged. This region is flat, but the terrain gives way to rolling hills in southern Logan County, and the river begins to broaden noticeably. From this point down to Dayton, the Great Miami changes little, remaining a pleasant Class I stream, flowing through farming country with occasional towns and farm-houses in many areas. There are few sharp turns, some shoals but no rapids, and the river is generally too wide for strainers to present a problem for anyone with a modicum of control. (Infrequent flood-control dams on this stretch can all be portaged easily.)

The sections of the river in Shelby and Miami counties are probably the most interesting. The river is bigger and more enjoy-able here than in Logan County, perhaps because of the bigger hills and more frequent woodlots. The river forks around more islands in these counties, its course is not so straight, and it seems more natural.

All of the Miami north of Dayton, together with several of the short rural sections downstream between Middletown and Hamilton, and Hamilton and Cleves, offer pleasant Class I cruising with scenery ranging from fair to pretty in spring, summer, and fall.

Historically, the Great Miami ranks with the Cuyahoga as two of the more abused waterways in the state. In recent years, however,

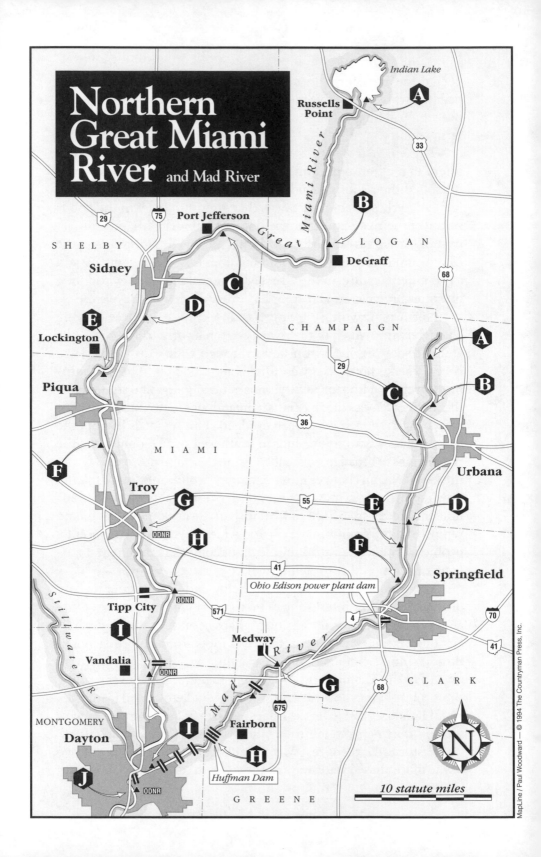

Northern Great Miami River and Mad River

Indian Lake

Russells Point

Great Miami River

A

33

B

S H E L B Y

Port Jefferson

L O G A N

C

DeGraff

Sidney

D

68

E

Lockington

C H A M P A I G N

Piqua

29

A

B

36

M I A M I

C

F

Troy

Urbana

G

55

E

D

ODNR

H

41

F

Ohio Edison power plant dam

Springfield

Stillwater R.

ODNR

Tipp City

571

70

I

Medway

Mad River

4

41

Vandalia

ODNR

G

68

C L A R K

675

MONTGOMERY

I

Fairborn

Dayton

H

J

Huffman Dam

ODNR

G R E E N E

N

10 statute miles

MapLine / Paul Woodward — © 1994 The Countryman Press, Inc.

significant progress has been made in cleaning up both rivers. As the river's water quality has improved, aquatic wildlife has increased. Bass fishing is very good at spots on the Great Miami, and anglers are once again beginning to take substantial numbers of sauger from this river, especially in the winter and early spring months.

Great Miami River

Counties:	Logan, Shelby, Miami, Montgomery, Warren, Butler, Hamilton
USGS Quads:	Russells Point, De Graff, Port Jefferson, Sidney, Piqua East, Piqua West, Troy, Tipp City, Dayton North, Dayton South, Miamisburg, Franklin, Middletown, Trenton, Hamilton, Greenhills, Shandon, Addyston, Hooven, Lawrenceburg (KY)
Difficulty:	International Class I
Hazards/Portages:	Numerous dams
Game-fish Species:	Smallmouth bass, largemouth bass, sauger
Additional Info:	Butler County Sheriff's Dept. (513) 867-5700

Access Point	Section	River Miles	Shuttle Miles
A. Indian Lake State Park in Russells Point	A–B	12	11
B. OH 508 bridge in De Graff	B–C	7.5	8.5
C. Port Jefferson roadside park N of town off OH 47	C–D	11.5	13.5
D. East Lockington Rd. bridge (closed) and Miami River Rd.	D–E	6.5	6
E. Piqua-Lockington Rd. bridge S of Lockington	E–F	8	6
F. Farrington-Peterson Rd. bridge	F–G	6.5	7
G. OH 41 bridge in Troy	G–H	6.5	6.5
H. OH 571 bridge	H–I	8	12
I. Taylorsville Reserve off OH 40 in Vandalia, access river right below dam	I–J	11.5	10
J. River's Edge Park in downtown Dayton, access river left below dam	J–K	13.5	12

K. Old OH 725 bridge in Miamisburg	K–L	9	9
L. Miami River Preserve off OH 73 in Middletown	L–M	15.5	16
M. Millikin Rd. (Township Rd. 278) off OH 4 NE of Hamilton	M–N	5	6.5
N. Combs Park by Two Mile Dam in Hamilton, river right	N–O	11.5	10
O. Miami River Rd. bridge SE of Venice	O–P	6.5	5
P. East Miami River Rd. W of New Baltimore	P–Q	12	9.5
Q. OH 50 bridge and Valley Junction Rd. in Cleves, access river right at low water	Q–R	6.5	6
R. Shawnee Lookout County Park off River Rd. SW of Cleves, access river left			

FOURMILE CREEK

Fourmile Creek begins in the silt-laden waters of Acton Lake at Hueston Woods State Park just north of the quaint little college town of Oxford. From here Fourmile Creek winds quickly through the hills and farms of Butler County before reaching its confluence with the Great Miami in Hamilton. The southern one-third of the stream, from Fourmile Creek Park to Hamilton, has traditionally been the most frequently run, for the stream is bigger here and less seasonal.

Upper stretches of the Fourmile provide scenic wet-weather paddling in winter and early spring, with a quick current and enough tight turns and obstacles in the form of logjams and uprooted trees to keep you alert. You'll come across the remnants of a number of old low-head dams on Fourmile Creek, none of which should present hazards. Stay alert on the upper reaches for strainers, fences, and the occasional proprietary landowner. If you opt to take out on the Great Miami at Combs-Jaycees' Memorial Park, hug the right bank immediately after the confluence. The dam just downstream is dangerous.

Fourmile Creek

Counties: Butler

USGS Quads: Oxford, Millville, Hamilton

Difficulty: International Class I

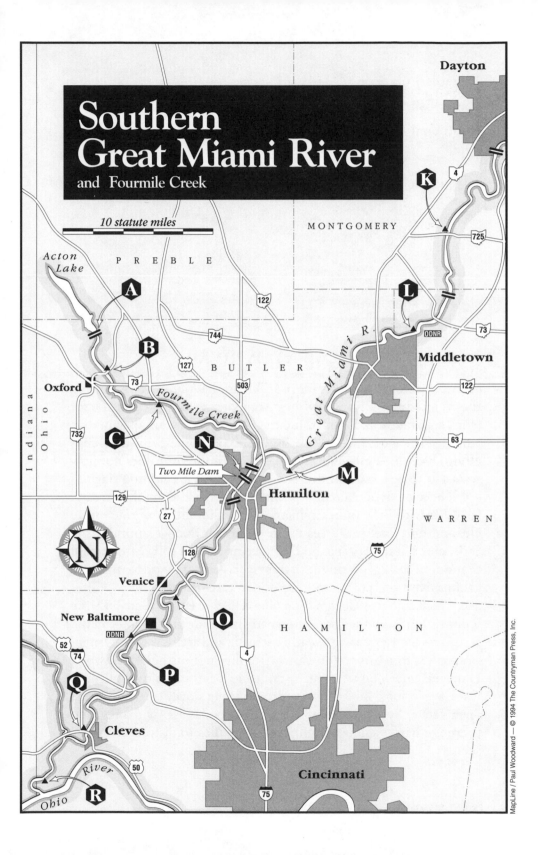

Hazards/Portages:	Deadfalls, fences
Game-fish Species:	Smallmouth bass
Additional Info:	Hueston Woods State Park (513) 523-6347

Access Point	Section	River Miles	Shuttle Miles
A. Dam at Acton Lake	A–B	3.5	4
B. Howell Park off Bonham Rd. NE of Oxford	B–C	7.5	6
C. OH 177 bridge S of Darrtown	C–N	10.5	10
N. Combs-Jaycees' Memorial Park on Great Miami River off US 127, N edge of Hamilton			

STILLWATER RIVER

The Stillwater River is no more still than the Mad River is mad or the Whitewater River is white—someone with a propensity for irony apparently named all Ohio rivers except those left with Native American names. In early spring, especially, the Stillwater clips along at a comparatively fast rate, although the river does not flow so fast as to be hazardous for beginners unless it's at flood stage.

The wide floodplain that prohibits residence along this stream, together with little or no industry, make the Stillwater one of the cleanest and prettiest streams in western Ohio. Thanks to the Stillwater's designation as an Ohio scenic river, it's likely to remain that way. The biggest threat to this river—as is the case for many of Ohio's rivers—is pollution from agricultural runoff.

The scenic river designation takes effect at Riffle Road in Darke County, but from that point downstream almost to Covington the Stillwater is strictly a wet-weather stream, and access is with permission only. From Covington on down to the huge earthen Englewood Dam at Englewood Reserve, just outside Dayton, the river changes little, averaging 60–80 feet in width, winding slowly through a wide farm valley. Sycamores and other hardwoods line the banks, and there are hardly enough tight turns or riffles to distract from the scenery.

There are several low-head dams on the Stillwater, most of them in the early or latter stages of washing out. Two of these are rock dams haphazardly constructed by local gravel companies: one is just downstream from the Fenner Road bridge, south of Pleasant Hill; the other is just inside the Montgomery County line, downstream from an old milldam. Both are loose conglomerations of concrete and stone, 15–20 feet wide and sloping downstream. Over the years channels have been worn through these dams that can be run by intermediate paddlers if sufficient water is running through them. Scout carefully, and keep in mind that a spill could mean a tumble over jagged rocks and spikes of concrete nastier than any natural formation you are likely to encounter. Both dams can be easily portaged on either bank.

You may also encounter the remnants of a conventional low-head dam, downstream from the Falknor Road bridge, and a gristmill dam (mentioned previously) just inside Montgomery County. As of this writing, both dams can be safely navigated at high water. However, the 8-foot power dam at West Milton is a mandatory portage. All these dams are clearly visible and audible and can easily be portaged, so you needn't hesitate to take the kids, dogs, or grandma down the Stillwater.

Stillwater River lives up to its name near its confluence with Greenville Creek.
[Jim Steiger photo]

Be alert for anglers wading the stream, especially in spring and early summer. The Stillwater is known for some of the best smallmouth bass fishing in the state.

The marsh and wetlands of the 1,075-acre Englewood Reserve at the dam in Englewood provide an interesting finish to a trip down the Stillwater. Depending on the season, you're almost sure to find yourself paddling among great blue herons or flocks of Canada geese, or both. Camping is available here, but permits must first be obtained from the Dayton—Montgomery County Park District.

Stillwater River

Counties:	Miami, Montgomery
USGS Quads:	Pleasant Hill, West Milton, Trotwood, Dayton North
Difficulty:	International Class I
Hazards/Portages:	Low-head dams, power dam
Game-fish Species:	Smallmouth bass
Additional Info:	Barefoot Canoes (513) 698-4351

Access Point	Section	River Miles	Shuttle Miles
A. Range Line Rd. bridge NW of Covington	A–B	3.5	4
B. Bird sanctuary at Falknor Rd. bridge and OH 48	B–C	2	2
C. Blankenship Sanctuary W of OH 48	C–D	4	5
D. OH 718 bridge W of Pleasant Hill	D–E	4	4
E. Fenner Rd. bridge N of Ludlow Falls	E–F	6	4
F. West Milton Park off Washington St. in West Milton	F–G	8	10
G. Englewood Reserve off US 40 N of Dayton			

GREENVILLE CREEK

From its confluence with Dismal Creek about halfway between Union City and Greenville, Greenville Creek provides seasonal paddling through most of Darke County, until it converges with the

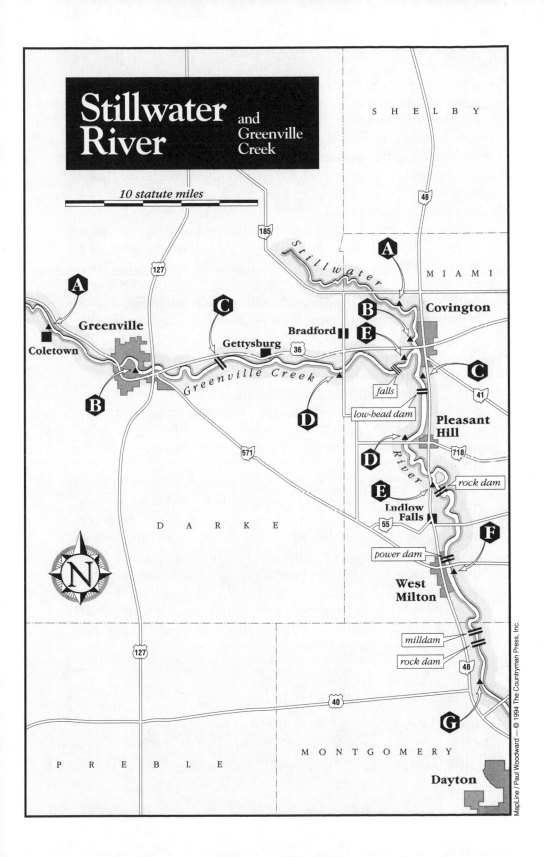

Stillwater River and Greenville Creek

10 statute miles

SHELBY

48

Stillwater

A

B

Covington

MIAMI

A

Greenville

127

185

C

Bradford

E

Gettysburg

36

Coletown

B

Greenville Creek

D

falls

low-head dam

C

41

Pleasant
Hill

D

571

River

718

E

rock dam

Ludlow
Falls

55

F

power dam

West
Milton

milldam

rock dam

48

N

DARKE

127

40

G

PREBLE

MONTGOMERY

Dayton

MapLine / Paul Woodward — © 1994 The Countryman Press, Inc.

Stillwater River at Covington. Darke County is near the heart of some of Ohio's best farm country, which is to say that with the exception of some gently rolling hills around Greenville and Covington, terrain ranges from flat to flatter still. Normally clear and sparkling, this bucolic little stream varies in width from 10 to 60 or more feet, with sycamores, oaks, and walnut trees lining the low banks and occasionally intertwining overhead.

Most paddlers put in at Greenville Park, where there is good public access and parking, and take out in Covington or one of several bridge crossings before Covington. You might want to investigate the creek upstream from Greenville if you're interested in a short trip and water levels are high, in which case Greenville Park is a good take-out. If you'd rather avoid the traffic, crowds, levees, and urban paddling in general, put in downstream from Greenville.

Shortly before Covington the bottom drops out from Greenville Creek; in the space of 50–60 yards the streambed descends 20–25 feet. The drop starts as a gentle slope marked by small shelves reaching only partway across the stream—these are easy enough to pick your way through. Then comes a falls of 4 feet or so, a shelf barely long enough for a canoe, followed immediately by another drop of 5 to 6feet.

We've paddled this area on two separate occasions; unfortunately, low water levels made running the falls clearly impossible on both. We cursed the low water and scouted carefully from both banks, conjecturing at length on the possibilities that might be afforded by higher water. Undoubtedly, running this section has been attempted; whether successfully or not we have been unable to determine. In any case it's important to note that the Darke County Paddlers, who have been paddling this stream for years, always portage around these falls. If you're not an experienced white-water paddler, don't even think about running them.

Greenville Creek

Counties: Darke, Miami

USGS Quads: Ansonia, Greenville West, Greenville
                       East, Gettysburg, Pleasant Hill

Difficulty: International Class I

Hazards/Portages: Deadfalls, dam, falls near Covington

Game-fish Species: Smallmouth bass

Additional Info: Bear's Mill and Pottery (513) 548-5112

Access Point	Section	River Miles	Shuttle Miles
A. County Rd. 26 in Coletown	A–B	7	6
B. Park in Greenville off Wilson Dr.	B–C	6	5
C. Arcanum-Bears Mill Rd. bridge W of Gettysburg	C–D	7.5	7
D. OH 721 bridge S of Bradford	D–E	5.5	5
E. Gettysburg Rd. bridge W of Covington			

MAD RIVER

The Mad River belies its name. You'll find no Painted Rocks or Turn-Back Canyons on this Class I stream, which flows from the high plains of Logan County in west central Ohio to the heavily industrialized Miami River Valley at Dayton. The long, straight course of the Mad's upper reaches is the only remaining evidence that the stream was channelized many years ago. Anyone with an eye for pastoral beauty will quickly see why the Mad River, particularly the northern stretch from Lippincott Road near Urbana to just above Springfield, is one of Ohio's most popular canoeing streams. Low but steep banks and a canopy formed by sycamores and cottonwoods leaning overhead lend a feeling of intimacy to this small, spring-fed stream, which looks like—and is—trout water, boasting excellent fishing for brown trout for anglers with fly rods or light spinning tackle. (The best trout fishing is in the area near Urbana. Farther downstream, approaching Springfield, the Mad is noted for its smallmouth bass fishing, and for over 50 years a Mad River smallmouth held the state record for the largest smallmouth caught in Ohio.)

The feeling of intimacy on the Mad is heightened by the narrow channel, with banks 20–30 feet apart in most places and sun-dappled water that runs cool and crystal clear year-round. The stream is small, but the unusually high groundwater storage of this region keeps even the uppermost reaches of the stream flowing at fairly consistent depths.

A peek beyond the banks lined in summer with black willows, fox grapes, and wildflowers will reveal that the upper Mad flows through a wide, flat plain of cornfields and wheat fields, interspersed here and there by huge old oaks and locust trees, gradually giving way to hills that roll gently off over the horizon.

Numerous access points make trip planning easy, but despite the easy access and the numerous liveries operating on the Mad, the stream is seldom so crowded as to spoil the sense of privacy. While the land bordering the river is private, several of the canoe liveries can arrange for streamside camping.

Although local paddlers sometimes canoe the section of the Mad immediately north of the Lippincott Road access, this is not recommended because of limited access and occasional fences across the river.

As the Mad approaches Springfield it begins to flatten out and loses the appearance of a trout stream. The water is warmer and less clear, and vegetation along the banks is increasingly sparse.

Just after the US 40 bridge and the confluence with Buck Creek west of Springfield is the Ohio Edison Dam, which must be portaged. From Springfield south, the Mad flows through heavily populated areas and never escapes the sound of traffic on nearby highways. A huge earthen monolith called Huffman Dam, near Wright-Patterson Air Force Base, must be portaged if you wish to paddle the river down to Eastwood City Park in Dayton, just before it empties into the Great Miami. (A map of the Mad River is on page 148.)

Mad River

Counties:	Champaign, Clark, Greene, Montgomery
USGS Quads:	Northville, Urbana West, Springfield, Donnelsville, Yellow Springs, Fairborn, Dayton North
Difficulty:	International Class I
Hazards/Portages:	Strainers, deadfalls, dams
Game-fish Species:	Brown trout Champaign County and north; smallmouth bass Clark County and south

Additional Info: Rainbow Adventures (513) 322-1432;
Morgan's Mad River Outpost
(513) 882-6925

Access Point	Section	River Miles	Shuttle Miles
A. Lippincott Rd. bridge	A–B	3.5	4.5
B. OH 29 bridge N of Urbana	B–C	4.5	6
C. US 36 bridge W of Urbana	C–D	6.5	11
D. County Line Rd. bridge	D–E	2	2
E. Tremont City Rd. bridge	E–F	4	5
F. St. Paris Pike bridge S of Eagle City	F–G	13	15
G. Spangler Rd. bridge SE of Medway	G–H	9.5	9
H. Huffman Reserve off Lower Valley Rd./ Huffman Dam Rd. in Fairborn	H–I	5.5	6
I. Deeds Park off Deeds Park and Webster roads at confluence with Great Miami			

LITTLE MIAMI RIVER

The upper two-thirds or so of the Little Miami River, flowing through Clark, Greene, and Warren counties, represents Ohio's first federal wild and scenic river. The Little Miami is considered by many to be the most scenic, pastoral stream in the state, although sections of it are often crowded on summer weekends. Generally a pleasant Class I river suitable for families with children, the Little Miami shows unusual variety in its 105-mile course from just south of Springfield to its confluence with the Ohio, meandering through an alternating landscape of corn-fields and tall wooded hills more typical of—although less rugged than—those of eastern Ohio. The exception to this is Clifton Gorge, near the headwaters of the Little Miami. The Clifton Gorge State Nature Preserve is off-limits to paddlers. (If you're putting in just downriver from Clifton Gorge, you might enjoy the short drive up to this most scenic part of the river to see why it's off-limits. Picture a stream with a steep gradient and several sharp dropoffs funneled through 75-foot vertical cliffs little more than a paddle's length apart in places, and you'll have a good idea.)

Contestants start the canoeing leg of the annual Little Miami Triathlon near Fort Ancient.

The access closest to the Clifton Gorge area is in John Bryan State Park on OH 370. A 3-mile section from here to just below the Jacoby Road launch is designated scenic, indicating that although it is not a wilderness area, surroundings are basically natural. Terrain in this area consists primarily of steep, wooded hills; the river itself is, as you might expect, smaller and more intimate here than farther downstream. This section of the river also tends to be less crowded, since few liveries offer excursions starting this far upstream.

From just above US 68 to the Caesars Creek launch, the Little Miami is again designated scenic. The stream begins widening here to 80 or more feet and forks occasionally around sandbars and small islands. There are more farms and other signs of civilization on this part of the river, including houses along the bank in places.

From Caesars Creek to Foster, just above the Hamilton County line, the Little Miami is designated scenic. The Hamilton County section flows near the heavily populated suburbs east of Cincinnati but is not nearly so urban as a glance at the map might suggest. Hills rise more steeply here than in most of Warren County, as the Little Miami approaches the Ohio River Valley. Cornfields are still numerous along the banks, and the river is bigger and a little pushier, forking more often around islands and sandbars, with occasional wide shoals making for Class I+ paddling when the river is running high. Nonetheless, low flow rates and high daytime temperatures can combine during the late summer months to raise the bacteria count to unacceptably high levels in the Hamilton County stretches of this stream.

Those who prefer to avoid weekend crowds can generally do so by paddling the extreme northern section or Hamilton County stretch of the river. Another option, however, is to paddle in the off-season. You can have the stream nearly all to yourself and enjoy the kind of pastoral serenity for which the Little Miami is justifiably noted.

Those interested in float fishing will find that the Little Miami offers a smorgasbord of fishing opportunities. Fishing for smallmouth bass, white bass, and panfish is very good in the spring and fall for most of the length of this popular stream. Within 8 or 10 miles of the Ohio, the Little Miami gets a good early-spring spawning of sauger and white bass. Try small white jigs with grubs, or small white spinners, in the pools below riffles for sauger and white bass.

Little Miami River

Counties:	Greene, Warren, Hamilton
USGS Quads:	Clifton, Yellow Springs, Xenia, Bellbrook, Waynesville, Oregonia, Pleasant Plain, South Lebanon, Mason, Madeira, Cincinnati East, Cincinnati West, Covington
Difficulty:	International Class I
Hazards/Portages:	Dams, strainers
Game-fish Species:	Smallmouth bass, white bass
Additional Info:	John Bryan State Park (513) 767-1274; canoe liveries (see Appendix B)

Access Point	Section	River Miles	Shuttle Miles
A. Launch at Jacoby Rd. bridge (closed) off US 68 S of Yellow Springs, access river right	A–B	2.5	3
B. US 68 bridge N of Xenia	B–C	4.5	6
C. Glen Thompson Reserve on US 35 and North Valley Rd. W of Xenia	C–D	6	6.5

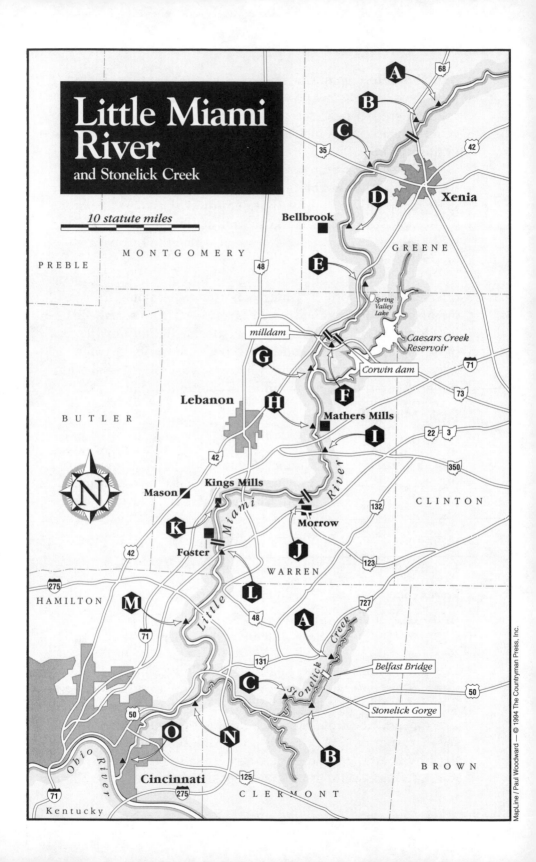

Little Miami River
and Stonelick Creek

10 statute miles

PREBLE

MONTGOMERY

GREENE

Xenia

Bellbrook

Spring
Valley
Lake

Caesars Creek
Reservoir

milldam

Corwin dam

Lebanon

BUTLER

Mathers Mills

Mason

Kings Mills

CLINTON

N

Morrow

Foster

WARREN

HAMILTON

Belfast Bridge

Stonelick Gorge

Cincinnati

Ohio River

BROWN

Kentucky

CLERMONT

MapLine / Paul Woodward — © 1994 The Countryman Press, Inc.

D. Mill Rd. bridge near Bellbrook	D–E	8.5	8
E. Roxanna–New Burlington Rd. bridge	E–F	6	7.5
F. Below Corwin dam on Corwin Rd., access river left	F–G	4	3.5
G. Caesars Creek access on Corwin Rd.	G–H	5.5	5
H. Wilmington Rd. bridge at Mathers Mills	H–I	2	4.5
I. Fort Ancient access at OH 350	I–J	5	5
J. Halls Creek access at Kibbey Ave. in Morrow	J–K	7	6
K. Grandin Rd. bridge at Kings Mills (steep access)	K–L	3.5	3.5
L. Glen Island access on County Rd. 10 in Foster	L–M	8	10
M. Lake Isabella Park N of Miamiville, river right	M–N	8.5	8
N. Little Miami Adventures off Bottom Rd. S of Millford	N–O	9.5	13
O. Mogrish Rec Center at US 52, Canoe Lane W of Mt. Washington, access river left			

STONELICK CREEK

Stonelick Creek is a tributary of the East Fork of the Little Miami River. It lies almost entirely within the boundaries of Clermont County, stretching from the county's northeast corner to a confluence with the East Fork near Perintown.

With a drainage basin of only 77 square miles, Stonelick is smaller than any other stream included in this guide. That small drainage basin, coupled with a precipitous gradient, keeps the streambed practically dry for most of each year. In fact, while there are no gauging stations along its roughly 30-mile length and historical water-flow data is nonexistent, it's safe to say that Stonelick is only rarely runnable.

Understandably enough, the characteristic lack of water has kept this stream relatively unknown, even among local paddlers. A drive over any of several bridges that cross the creek typically reveals nothing more than a string of potholes tenuously connected by a barely perceptible trickle of water flowing over and between broken slabs of bedrock that litter the stream channel. Nevertheless, in recent years this creek has been discovered by a handful of southwestern Ohio's white-water addicts looking for a fix close to home.

A Stonelick Creek ford: At low water the road surface is dry and paddlers must portage. At high water hydraulics can form on the downstream edge, much like those below low-head dams.

What they've found is an 8-mile torture track lying at the bottom of a jagged cut in the limestone bedrock of southwestern Ohio. The channel is narrow and often partially obstructed by deadfalls. Stream-wide ledges predominate, and between them the stream bottom falls away at an average of 30 feet per mile. In a 3-mile section of the stream known as Stonelick Gorge (the section between the Belfast Road and OH 132 bridges), the gradient increases to 55 feet per mile, which, when the rain gods oblige, makes this the high-speed lane.

Occasionally a summer thunderstorm will dump just enough rain on the watershed to make the stream runnable. At these water levels (1 to 2 feet at the OH 131 bridge), the gorge is a challenging technical run. But on those rare occasions when the heavy spring rains combine with snowmelt to raise the stream level to 5 feet or more, the Stonelick Gorge reverberates with a liquid thunder.

At the OH 131 bridge the white-water run on Stonelick begins with a sweeping left turn against a cut right bank about 30 feet high. Deadfalls and strainers are an ever-present danger here, and in Stonelick's narrow streambed they merit a paddler's keenest vigilance. As the stream twists from left to right, dropping steadily, it cuts its way through high shale banks dotted with hardwoods and conifers. Ledges, surfing holes, and continuous 2- to 3-foot waves (punctuated by an occasional 5-footer at the bases of the bigger drops) characterize this portion of the run. Undercut ledges (together with strainers) present a constant entrapment potential, but the first 3 miles are otherwise tame in comparison to what follows. If you have problems here, you should consider walking out at the Belfast Road bridge. (The bridge has been closed, and there is no public access, absent an emergency, at this point.)

Stonelick Gorge begins just past the Belfast Road bridge. At Duckling Drop (a ledge followed by a keeper hydraulic, runnable only through a 5-foot chute on river right), the pitch and speed of the stream increase dramatically. The next ½ mile is characterized by large reactionary waves crisscrossing the stream from both banks. Johnson's Ledge (a river-wide, 6-foot drop followed by an immensely powerful hydraulic not too facetiously known as The Hole Nobody Surfs) is the next major drop and is a mandatory portage.

The following half-mile brings more of the large reactionary waves, with one added twist: the stream is now banked by slick, 50-foot-high mud-and-clay cliffs. During periods of heavy rain these cliffs can become unstable, with mud slides crashing down into the stream. As the channel straightens between the unstable cliffs, and the reactionary waves lose intensity, the power of the current is transformed into pure velocity, and boaters find themselves in some screamin' flatwater.

At low water levels it is possible to take out at the OH 132 bridge. The banks on both sides here are undercut, however; at high water levels, that fact coupled with the speed of the current here makes it much easier to continue downstream to the Bensen Road ford to take out.

Stonelick Creek

Counties:	Clermont
USGS Quads:	Goshen
Difficulty:	International Class III (IV); this is a serious white-water run for accomplished paddlers using specialized equipment and taking due precaution

Hazards/Portages:	Strainers, falls, large reactionary waves, keeper hydraulic at Johnson's Ledge
Game-fish Species:	Smallmouth bass near the confluence with the Little Miami River; unfortunately, the high-water conditions that make this stream paddleable also make it unfishable—you'll have to wade it to fish it

Access Point	Section	River Miles	Shuttle Miles
A. OH 131 bridge W of Newtonsville	A–B	6	5.5
B. OH 132 bridge **Mandatory Portage**	B–C	2	5
C. Benson Rd. ford			

WHITE OAK CREEK

White Oak Creek is a small but intense stream that flows through the scenic hill country of western Brown County and empties into the Ohio River south of Georgetown. This relatively little-known stream affords southwestern Ohio paddlers some of the prettiest and, at high water levels, most exciting paddling in the state.

This is not a stream for novices. At minimum runnable water levels the White Oak is frustratingly technical; at high water levels paddlers must contend with violent, high standing waves, several intimidating souse holes, and at least two falls in the space of a very fast 10-mile run. There are few eddies in which paddlers can plan strategies or rest.

Scouting the stream at high water levels is very difficult, and the stream is pushy, offering little time to think or react. Under optimum white-water conditions (approaching flood stage), the White Oak tests the limits of navigability for open boats piloted by any but expert canoeists. Even if you're a decked boater, however, you might want to think twice about running this stream if you don't have a bomb-proof roll. In any case, extra flotation is a must; the speed of the current, the absence of eddies, and high, steep bluffs in some places make rescue efforts difficult.

A spill more than likely means a long swim and quite possibly a lost boat.

Groundwater retention in the White Oak Valley is quite low. Except for the northernmost section, the stream has carved its way through the steep hills of the area to a shale and limestone bed, meaning that the White Oak goes up and down quickly. This is especially true in summer, but you'll want to keep it in mind any time you put in on this stream. The trick is to call the Georgetown Waterworks at the last possible moment before departing to ask how much water is going over the dam. They usually say all of it, but if pressed are quite friendly about walking down to take a look at the gauge the Miami Sierra Club has painted on the upstream side of the dam. (The waterworks is staffed 24 hours a day, but employees do leave for meals.) If there is less than 8 inches of water flowing over the dam, or if the water level is near 8 inches and falling, don't make the drive.

The northernmost put-in we recommend is at the Bethel–New Hope Road bridge just south of New Hope and immediately downstream from the Sterling Run–White Oak confluence. The gradient is comparatively slight here, and for the next 5 miles or so the White Oak flows slowly over a soft, silty bottom. The terrain is less rugged—and less scenic—than farther downstream.

The whitewater run on White Oak Creek has many 3-foot drops and ledges just like this.

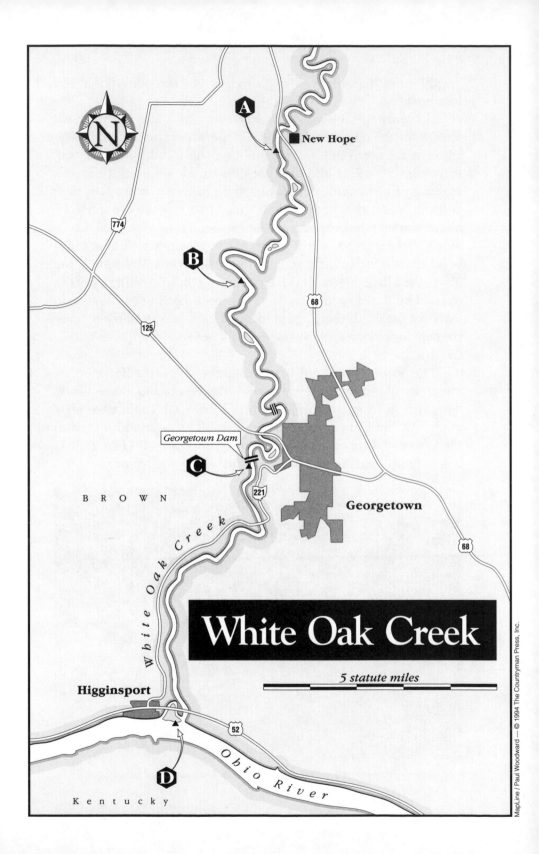

Near the White Oak Valley Road bridge the gradient picks up; the stream runs more quickly over a rocky shale and limestone bed, and the previously flat countryside of the upper White Oak Valley begins to give way to the steep, rugged hills common to the Ohio River Valley. Strata of limestone and shale are exposed along the banks, and the stream forks frequently around sandbars and small islands.

Less than 4 miles downstream from the White Oak Valley Road bridge is a large and aptly named souse hole called First Drop. If you are alert and see it—or hear it—on time, you can sideslip the worst of it to the left. If not, you'll have little time after digging your way out of the hydraulic to eddy out and bail before finding yourself right on top of another, only slightly less intimidating drop. From here on down to OH 125, the White Oak is a joy ride as it thunders down a steep incline (turning at one point against the face of a 100-foot cliff) and roars over boulders and limestone ledges in a maelstrom of spray and high turbulent, standing waves. Near the end of this stretch, less than 1 mile from the OH 125 bridge, is Supershelf, a river-wide ledge that should be approached with caution, because the velocity of the current here can make back ferrying difficult. Hug the right bank and scout this falls carefully. A dirt road makes portaging easy, should you choose to exercise that option. The falls is most often run on river left, alongside the steep bluff.

A rock garden under the OH 125 bridge requires some skillful maneuvering when the stream is running low; at high water levels this rapids is less technical, but strong reactionary waves make it squirrely. Stay alert when you see the bridge.

From the bridge down to the Georgetown Dam, there are several Class II rapids and one chute with high standing waves, although these are not so high as those encountered upstream.

Approach the Georgetown Dam with caution, and don't attempt to run it. Below the dam jagged fragments of concrete and twisted steel rods await the foolhardy.

White Oak Creek

Counties:	Brown
USGS Quads:	Hamersville, Higginsport
Difficulty:	International Class III (IV)

Hazards/Portages:	Falls, dam, hydraulics, high standing waves
Game-fish Species:	Smallmouth bass, largemouth bass (near mouth)
Additional Info:	Georgetown Waterworks (513) 378-6768

Access Point	Section	River Miles	Shuttle Miles
A. New Hope Rd.–White Oak Station Rd. by covered bridge	A–B	5.5	5
B. White Oak Valley Rd. bridge (access difficult)	B–C	7	6
C. Water treatment plant by dam on OH 221 W of Georgetown	C–D	7.5	7.5
D. White Oak Creek launch ramp on Ohio at mouth of White Oak			

OHIO BRUSH CREEK

Ohio Brush Creek starts south of Hillsboro in Highland County. It is joined by Lost Fork about 8 miles south of town, but not until it is south of Belfast can Ohio Brush Creek be called anything but a brook. From here this small, usually clear-running stream flows south to the Ohio River, bisecting Adams County and some of the most beautiful and relatively unspoiled country in the state.

The landscape consists of rugged unglaciated hills interspersed with wide, flat valleys. As if in imitation, the stream consists of slow pools separated by small limestone ledges. Sycamores predominate along the banks, with occasional stands of evergreen. Shale and limestone cliffs form the bank in spots; the shale weathers quickly to a sticky blue-gray clay near the water line.

A gentle Class I stream, the Ohio Brush Creek is canoeable south of Belfast except in later summer, fall, or following any long, dry period. Unfortunately—or fortunately, depending on your perspective—access is limited on this stream. There are three public access points, but two are near the Ohio River where the creek is backed up in the Ohio River Valley. (Ohio Brush Creek starts backing up a few miles south of OH 125 and quickly becomes wide, muddy, and flat. This section is open to powerboat traffic from the Ohio.)

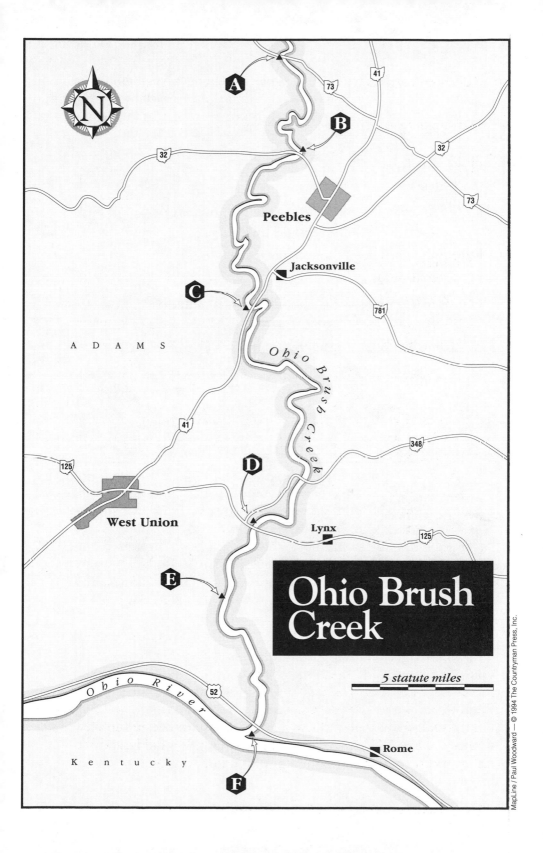

Ohio Brush Creek offers good smallmouth bass fishing in spring, early summer, and fall. As the stream begins backing up from the Ohio, spotted and largemouth bass are present as well, along with white bass and panfish.

Ohio Brush Creek

Counties: Adams

USGS Quads: Belfast, Sinking Spring, Peebles, Lynx, Concord

Difficulty: International Class I

Hazards/Portages: Strainers

Game-fish Species: Smallmouth bass, largemouth bass (near mouth), sauger

Additional Info: Elmore Enterprises (513) 544-3676

Access Point	Section	River Miles	Shuttle Miles
A. OH 73 bridge (fair access)	A–B	7.5	8
B. OH 32 bridge	B–C	10	7.5
C. OH 41 bridge S of Jacksonville (fair access)	C–D	13	12
D. OH 125 bridge	D–E	3.5	4
E. Beasley Fork Rd. SW of Lynx, N of confluence with Beasley Fork	E–F	6	6
F. Ohio Brush Creek boat ramp off US 52 W of Rome			

Appendix A

White-Water Streams

Ohio is not noted for its white-water paddling. The streams listed below are generally well behaved, or, in a few instances, not navigable. But with sufficient water volume in spring, after heavy rains in summer, or as a result of dam releases, these streams offer some excellent white-water paddling, with difficulty ratings ranging from Class II on several streams to Class IV on others.

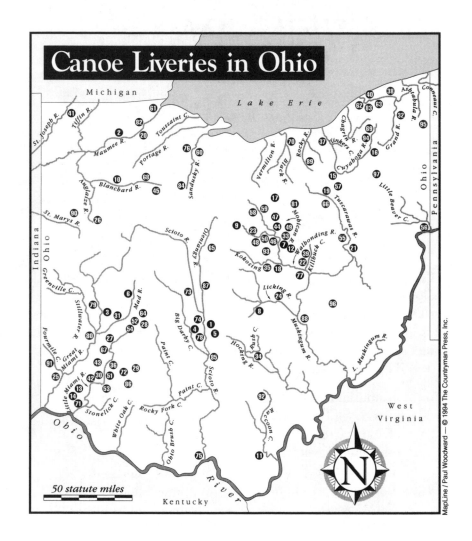

Canoe Liveries in Ohio

Michigan

Lake Erie

Indiana

Ohio

Pennsylvania

West Virginia

Kentucky

50 statute miles

Appendix B

Canoe Liveries

Canoe Liveries in Ohio

1   All Ohio Canoe Rental
    320 S. Admore Rd.
    Columbus 43209
    (614) 235-8296, 837-0327
    Scioto, Hocking, Licking rivers

2   Bad Creek Campground
    Rt. 2, Box 107
    Liberty Center 43532
    (419) 533-6732
    Maumee River

3   Barefoot Canoes
    3565 W. Frederick-Gingham Rd.
    Tipp City 45371
    (513) 698-4351
    Stillwater, Great Miami, Mad rivers

4   Big Darby Canoe Livery
    5761 Harrisburg-Georgesville Rd.
    Grove City 43123
    (614) 877-2193
    Big Darby Creek

5   Big Walnut Landing
    4464 Winchester Pike
    Columbus 43227
    (614) 837-0327, 235-8296
    Big Walnut Creek

6   Birch Bark Canoe Livery
    1455 River Rd.
    Urbana 43078-9381
    (513) 652-3493
    Mad River

7   Black Fork Kayak & Canoe
    Livery
    RD 2 (SR 3)
    Loudonville 44842
    (419) 994-4354
    *Black Fork, Clear Fork,
    Mohican rivers*

8   Blackhand Gorge Canoe Livery
    11101 Staddens Bridge Rd.
    Newark 43055
    (614) 763-4000
    Licking River

9   Blue Lagoon Canoe Livery
    1497 SR 97
    Butler 44842
    (419) 883-3888
    Clear Fork Mohican River

10 Bo Conn Canoe Livery
    705 N. Walnut
    Ottawa 45875
    (419) 523-6544
    Blanchard River

11 Bob Evans Farm
    Rt. 35, Box 330
    Rio Grande 45674
    (614) 245-5304
    Raccoon Creek

12 Brinkhaven Canoe Livery
    PO Box 277
    Brinkhaven 43006
    (614) 599-7848
    *Mohican, Walhonding,
    Muskingum rivers*

13 Bruce's Canoe Rental
    SR 48
    South Lebanon 45065
    (513) 494-2100
    Little Miami River

14 Bruce's Loveland Canoe Rental
    200 Taylor St.
    Loveland 45140
    (513) 683-4611
    Little Miami River

15 Burch's Landing
    354 Portage Lakes Dr.
    Akron 44319
    (216) 644-0234
    Cuyahoga River

16 Camp Hi Canoe Livery
    12068 Abbott Rd.
    Hiram 44234
    (216) 569-7621
    Cuyahoga River

17 Camp Toodik Resort Park &
    Canoe Livery
    7700 TR 462
    Loudonville 44842
    (419) 994-4350
    Lake Fork Branch, Mohican,
    Walhonding, Muskingum rivers

18 Campways of Ohio
    PO Box 38
    Walhonding 43843
    (614) 824-3220
    Mohican River

19 Canal Fulton Canoe Livery
    4075 Eastern Rd.
    Norton 44203
    (216) 658-2331
    Tuscarawas River

20 The Canoe Shop
    140 S. River Rd.
    Waterville 43566
    (419) 878-3700
    Maumee River

21 Carlisle Canoe Center
    2163 Goshen Rd. (SR 416)
    PO Box 161
    New Philadelphia 44663
    (216) 339-4010, 343-7633,
    339-3805
    Tuscarawas River

22 Casey's Recreational Center
    327 Main St.
    Coshocton 43812-1510
    (614) 622-4080
    Mohican River

23 Clear Fork Canoe Livery
    PO Box 247
    Butler 44822
    (419) 883-3601
    Clear Fork, Black Fork rivers

24 Dillon Lake Water Sports
    6275 Clay-Littick Dr.
    Nashport 43830
    (614) 453-7964, 1-800-640-7964
    Licking River

25 Ford Canal Canoe Livery
    Dept. of Parks & Recreation
    Ford Blvd.
    Hamilton 45013
    (513) 894-4194
    Great Miami River, Old Ford Canal

26 Ft. Amanda Livery
    Rt. 4 (Doughill Rd.)
    Cridersville 45806
    (419) 657-6782, 657-6917
    Auglaize River

27 Fyffe's Canoe Rental
    2750 Washington Mill Rd.
    Bellbrook 45305
    (513) 848-4812
    Little Miami River

28 Fyffe's Canoe Rental
    420 Upper Valley Pike
    Springfield 45502
    (513) 325-9069
    Upper Mad River

29 Gordon's Canoe Rental
9456 SR 350
Clarksville 45113
(513) 289-2792, 932-7117
Little Miami River

30 Gordon's Ft. Ancient
225 Corwin Rd.
Oregonia 45054
(513) 932-7117
Little Miami River

31 Gordon's Miami Shores Canoe
Rentals
5605 Lower Valley Pike
Donnelsville 45319
(513) 882-6925
Mad River

32 Grand River Canoe Livery
3825 Fobes Rd.
Rock Creek 44084
(216) 563-3486, 352-7400
Grand River

33 Hawkeye's Canoe Livery
Box 203-1-A
Loudonville 44842
(419) 994-3103
Mohican River

34 Hocking Valley Canoe Livery
31251 Chiefton Dr.
Logan 43138
(614) 385-8685, 385-2503
Hocking River

35 Howard Canoe Livery
23760 Coshocton Rd.
Howard 43028
(614) 599-7056
Kokosing River

36 I-71/Ft. Ancient Canoe Rental
I-71 & Warren Co. Rd. 7 (Exit
36)
Oregonia 45054
(513) 932-7117, 289-2797
Little Miami River

37 Keelhaulers Outfitters
30940 Lorain Rd.
North Olmstead 44070
(216) 779-4545
Cuyahoga River

38 Keniss's Grand River Camp &
Canoe
4680 SR 307
Geneva 44041
(216) 466-2320
Grand River

39 Kokosing Valley Camp & Canoe
25860 Coshocton Rd. (Rt. 36)
Howard 43028
(614) 599-7056
Kokosing River

40 Lake County Canoes
81 Elevator Ave.
Painesville 44077
(216) 352-7400
Grand River

41 Lazy River Campground
Rt. 1
Pioneer 43554
(419) 485-4411
St. Joseph River

42 Little Miami Canoe Rental
219 Mill St.
Morrow 45152
(513) 868-0541, 1-800-634-4277
Little Miami River

43 Little Miami River Canoe Rental
5380 Wilmington Rd.
Oregonia 45054
(513) 899-3616
Little Miami River

44 Loudonville Canoe Livery
424 W. Main St.
Loudonville 44842
(419) 994-4161
Black Fork, Mohican rivers

45 Millstream Canoe Livery
Hancock Park District
819 Park St.
Findlay 45840
(419) 422-1433, 422-7148, 423-6952
Blanchard River

46 Mohican Canoe Livery
SR 3, Box 263
Loudonville 44842
(419) 994-4097, 938-6083
Clear Fork, Mohican, Walhonding, Muskingum rivers

47 Mohican River Canoe Livery
PO Box 69
Perrysville 44864
(419) 994-4020
Mohican, Black Fork rivers

48 Mohican River Valley Canoe Livery
SR 3, Box 32
Loudonville 44842
(419) 994-5204
Black Fork, Mohican rivers

49 Mohican State Park Canoe Livery
130 Humm Ave.
Loudonville 44842
(419) 994-4135, 1-800-442-2663
Mohican River

50 Mohican Wilderness
SR 3 & Wally Rd.
Loudonville 44842
(614) 599-6741
Mohican River

51 Morgan's Ft. Ancient Canoe Livery
5701 SR 350
Oregonia 45054
(513) 932-7658, 899-2166
Little Miami River

52 Morgan's Mad River Outpost
5605 Lower Valley Pk.
Springfield 45506
(513) 882-6925
Mad River

53 Morrow Canoe Rental
SR 123
Morrow 45152
(513) 899-3616
Little Miami River

54 New World Expeditions
Xenia Ave.
Yellow Springs 45387
(513) 767-7221
Little Miami River

55 NTR Canoe Livery
SR 212, Box 203
Bolivar 44612
(216) 874-2002
Tuscarawas River

56 Ohio Canoe Tours
Rt. 170, Frederick Town Rd.
East Liverpool 43920
1-800-435-KANU,
(216) 497-5268
Little Beaver Creek

57 Ohio Canoe Tours
2894 Daisybrook St.
North Canton 44720
1-800-435-KANU,
(216) 497-5268
Little Beaver Creek

58 Pleasant Hill Canoe Livery
914 SR 39
Perrysville 44864
(419) 938-7777
Black Fork, Mohican, Walhonding, Muskingum rivers

59 Pleasant Valley Campsite
RR 2, Box 168
Loudonville 44842
(419) 994-4024
Mohican River

60 Portage Trail Canoe Livery
1773 S. River Rd.
Fremont 43420
(419) 334-2988
Sandusky River

61 Portage Trail Canoe Livery
5843 317th Street
Toledo 43611-2446
(419) 334-8100
Maumee River

62 Raccoon Run Canoe Rental
296 Normandy
Painesville 44077
(216) 354-0950
Grand River, Chagrin River,
Conneaut Creek

63 Raccoon Run Canoe Rental
1129 State Rd.
Harpersfield 44041
(216) 466-7414
Grand River, Chagrin River,
Conneaut Creek

64 Rainbow Adventure Canoe
Rental
1610 Upper Valley Pike
Springfield 45504
(513) 322-1432
Little Miami, Mad rivers

65 River Bend Camping & Canoeing
1092 Whetstone River Rd. South
Caledonia 43314
(614) 389-4179
Olentangy River

66 River Run Canoe Livery
219 Cherry St.
Canal Fulton 44614
(216) 854-3394
Tuscarawas River

67 River's Edge Canoe Livery
3928 State Route 42 S.
Waynesville 45068
(513) 862-4540
Little Miami River

68 Riverside Landing
c/o Hancock Park Dist.
819 Park St.
Findlay 45840
(419) 423-1902, 423-6952
Blanchard River

69 Riverside Park
13468 Main Market Rd.
Burton 44021
(216) 834-4337
Cuyahoga River

70 Romp's Water Port
5055 Liberty Ave.
Vermilion 44089
(216) 967-4342
Vermilion River

71 Scenic River Excursions
4595 Round Bottom Rd.
Cincinnati 45343
(513) 248-9610
Little Miami River

72 Scenic Route Campground &
Canoe Livery
9388 SR 350
Clarksville 45113
(513) 289-2797
Little Miami River

73 Schrock Canoes
2996 SR 257
Ostrander 43061-9410
Scioto River

74 Scioto Canoe Rental
675 London-Groveport Rd.
Lockbourne 43137
Scioto River

75 Shawnee Adventures
Friendship 45630-0110
(614) 353-8333
Scioto River

76 Tackle Box II
104 East State St.
Fremont 43420
(419) 334-4643
Sandusky River

77 Three Rivers Canoe Livery
US 36 & SR 83
Lake Park Rd.
Coshocton 43812
(614) 622-4080
Mohican, Walhonding, Muskingum,
Tuscarawas rivers

78 Trapper John's Canoe Livery
    7141 London-Groveport Rd.
    Grove City 43123
    (614) 877-4321
    Big Darby Creek

79 Treasure Island Canoe Adventures
    439 N. Elm St.
    Troy 45373
    (513) 339-5555
    Great Miami River

80 Twin Rivers Canoe Livery
    2808 N. Dixie Dr.
    Dayton 45414
    (513) 274-9310
    Great Miami River

81 Wally Camp Resort
    PO Box 120
    Loudonville 44842
    (419) 994-4828, 994-3629
    Mohican River

82 Waterville Outdoor World
    Canoe Livery
    205 Farnsworth Rd.
    Peddlers' Alley
    Waterville 43566
    (419) 878-1881
    Maumee River

83 Willow Grove Marina
    14217 Painesville-Warren Rd.
    Painesville 44077
    (216) 639-1265
    Grand River

84 Wyandot Canoe Livery
    503 Gamber Ct.
    Upper Sandusky 43351
    Sandusky River

State Parks with Liveries

85 A. W. Marion
    Circleville
    (614) 474-3386

86 Cowan Lake
    Clarksville
    (513) 289-2105

87 Delaware
    Delaware
    (614) 369-2761

88 Dillon
    Zanesville
    (614) 453-4377

89 Findlay
    Wellington
    (216) 647-4490

90 Grand Lake St. Marys
    St. Marys
    (419) 394-3611

91 Hueston Woods
    Oxford
    (513) 523-6347

92 Lake Hope
    Zaleski
    (614) 596-5253

93 Mohican
    Loudonville
    (419) 994-5323, 994-4290

94 Punderson
    Newbury
    (216) 564-2279

95 Pymatuning
    Andover
    (216) 293-6030

96 Salt Fork
    Cambridge
    (614) 439-3521

97 West Branch
    Ravenna
    (216) 296-3239

Appendix C

Canoeing and Kayaking Organizations

The following is a list of canoeing and kayaking organizations in Ohio, including the name and phone number of a person to contact for information about the group, the type of training programs each group offers, and, in some cases, the type of paddling the group tends to concentrate on. All clubs that do not offer formal training programs hastened to report that they do offer training on an informal basis, and all clubs welcome new members. Most of these clubs require annual dues, generally $10–$20.

Buckeye Canoe Club (North Canton)
    Don Myers
    2314 State Street NE
    Canton 44721
    (216) 877-2546
    Racing/no formal training program

Columbus AYH
   Mary Beth Lohse
   P.O. Box 2311
   Columbus 43223-0111
   (614) 891-6362
   Downriver paddling/formal training for all levels of paddling, including instructor training

Cleveland Sierra Club
   (216) 321-3711
   Sierra Clubs Main Office
   65 South Fourth Street
   Columbus 43215
   Downriver paddling/formal training for tandem canoeing, beginners and intermediates

Darke County Paddlers
   Harvey Mikesell
   (513) 996-5886
   Racing/no formal training program

Dayton Canoe Club
   Mike Frazier
   1020 Riverside Drive
   Dayton 45405
   (513) 277-9626
   Canoe sailing, flatwater paddling/no formal training

Keelhaulers (Northeastern Ohio)
   30940 Lorain Road
   N. Olmsted 44070
   (216) 248-4166
   Downriver paddling/formal training for intermediate to advanced white-water paddlers, kayak rolling

Madhatters (Northeastern Ohio)
   Roy Pratt
   221 Parrish Boulevard
   Conneaut 44030
   (216) 599-8717
   Racing/formal training in kayak rolling

Miami Group Sierra Club (Cincinnati)
(513) 841-0111
see Main Office address under
Cleveland Sierra Club, above
*Downriver paddling/formal training for tandem canoeing, begin-
ners and intermediates*

Wright-Patterson Outdoor Adventure Club (Dayton)
Rod Joblove
2845 Liberty-Ellerton Road
Dayton 45418
(513) 835-3268
Formal training for all skill levels, open and decked boats

More Info:

Department of Travel and Tourism (1-800-BUCKEYE)

American Red Cross (check your local white pages listing)

In addition to the above clubs, the Greater Cleveland Red Cross
conducts training programs for all skill levels, open and
decked boats, solo and tandem. Contact Jim Gorman at
(216) 243-3667.

Ohio Department of Natural Resources

Division of Watercraft District Offices

All district officers are certified canoe instructors and offer valuable resources and information for paddlers in their districts.

Central Office

Fountain Square—Building C/2
Columbus 43224
(614) 466-3686 or 466-7806

District I

830 Kinnear Road
Columbus 43212
(614) 265-7018

District II

1976 Buck Creek Lane
Springfield 45502
(513) 323-1582

District III

> 1225 Woodlawn Avenue
> Cambridge 43725
> (614) 439-4076

District IV

> 2756 S. Arlington Road
> Akron 44312
> (216) 644-2265

District V

> 8701 Lakeshore Blvd., N.E.
> Cleveland 44108
> (216) 361-1212

District VI

> 3916 East Perkins Avenue
> P.O. Box 213
> Huron 44839
>
> (419) 433-2782

District VII

> 10556 McKelvey Road
> Cincinnati 45240
> (513) 851-1755

Additional Info:

> Ohio Historic Canoe Route Association
> c/o Division of Watercraft
> Fountain Square
> Columbus, OH 43224
> (614) 265-6480

Appendix E

Glossary of Paddling Terms

Bottom. The stream bottoms described in this guide allude to what the paddler sees as opposed to the geological composition of the riverbed.

Bow. The front of a boat.

Broaching. A boat that is sideways to the current and usually out of control or pinned to an obstacle in the stream.

cfs. Cubic feet per second; an accurate method of expressing river flow in terms of function of flow and volume.

C-1. One-person, decked canoe equipped with a spray skirt; frequently mistaken for a kayak. The canoeist kneels in the boat and uses a single-bladed paddle.

C-2. A two-person, decked canoe; frequently mistaken for a two-person kayak.

Chute. A clear channel between obstructions that has faster current than the surrounding water.

Curler. A wave that curls or falls back on itself (upstream).

Deadfalls. Trees that have fallen into the stream, totally or partially obstructing it.

Decked boat. A completely enclosed canoe or kayak fitted with a spray skirt. When the boater is properly in place, this forms a nearly waterproof unit.

Downstream ferry. A technique for moving sideways in the current while facing downstream. Can also be done by "surfing" on a wave.

Downward erosion. The wearing away of the bottom of a stream by the current.

Drainage area. Officially defined as an area measured in a horizontal plane, enclosed by a topographic divide, from which direct surface runoff from precipitation normally drains by gravity into a stream above a specified point. In other words, this is an area that has provided the water on which you are paddling at any given time. Accordingly, the drainage area increases as you go downstream. The drainage basin of a river is expressed in square miles. (Also known as "watershed.")

Drop. Paddler's term for **Gradient.**

Dry dam. These are flood-control devices. They are generally constructed of earth with large gates at their bases that are only closed during flood conditions. Thus, there is no permanent impoundment behind a dry dam. Large concrete shute blocks below the gates make it unsafe to attempt to run dry dams.

Eddy. The water behind an obstruction in the current or behind a river bend. The water may be relatively calm or boiling and will flow upstream.

Eddy line. The boundary at the edge of an eddy between two currents of different velocity and direction.

Eddy out. *See* **Eddy turn.**

Eddy turn. Maneuver used to move into an eddy from the downstream current.

Eskimo roll. The technique used to upright an overturned decked canoe or kayak, by the occupant, while remaining in the craft. This is done by coordinated body motion and usually facilitated by the proper use of the paddle.

Expert boater. A person with extensive experience and good judgment who is familiar with up-to-date boating techniques, practical hydrology, and proper safety practices. An expert boater never paddles alone and always uses the proper equipment.

Falls. A portion of river where the water falls freely over a drop. This designation has nothing to do with hazard rating or difficulty. *See* **Rapids.**

Ferry. Moving sideways to the current facing either upstream or downstream.

Flotation. Additional buoyant materials (air bags, Styrofoam, inner tubes, etc.) placed in a boat to provide displacement of water and extra buoyancy in case of upset.

Grab loops. Loops (about 6 inches in diameter) of nylon rope or similar material attached to the bow and stern of a boat to facilitate rescue.

Gradient. The geographical drop of the river expressed in feet per mile.

Haystack. A pyramid-shaped standing wave caused by deceleration of current from underwater resistance.

Headward erosion. The wearing away of the rock strata forming the base of ledges or waterfalls by the current.

Heavy water. Fast current, large waves, usually associated with holes and boulders.

Hydraulic. General term for souse holes and back rollers, where there is a hydraulic jump (powerful current differential) and strong reversal current.

K-1. One-person, decked kayak equipped with spray skirt. In this guidebook, this category does not include nondecked kayaks. The kayaker sits in the boat with both feet extended forward. A double-bladed paddle is used.

Keeper. A souse hole or hydraulic with sufficient vacuum in its trough to hold an object (paddler, boat, log, etc.) that floats into it for an undetermined time. Extremely dangerous and to be avoided.

Lateral erosion. The wearing away of the sides or banks of a stream by the current.

Ledge. The exposed edge of a rock stratum that acts as a low, natural dam or as a series of such dams.

Lining. A compromise between portaging and running a rapids. By the use of a rope (line), a boat can be worked downstream from the shore.

Logjam. A jumbled tangle of fallen trees, branches, and sometimes debris that totally or partially obstructs a stream.

Low-head dam. These are small dams built for purposes other than water supply reservoirs. They can be as low as 6 inches or as high as 10 feet. They are usually constructed of concrete, though smaller ones are sometimes built with rock and timbers. Water flows over the entire top of the dam creating uniform, river-wide hydraulics at the dam's base that can be very dangerous.

Low-water bridge. A bridge across the river that barely clears the surface of the water or may even be awash; very dangerous for the paddler if in a fast current.

Low-water dam. These are low-head dams with a notch cut in the center so that water flows only through the notch at all times except when high water levels exist. At low water levels these dams are not as dangerous as standard low-head dams because the hydraulic at the base is not uniform nor river-wide. However, concrete baffles to reduce erosion, usually located below the notch, can cause severe damage to bodies and boats.

Permanent impoundment dam. Built for flood control, water supply, and recreation, these dams are designed so that no water flows over them. Obviously, they are not runnable.

Pool. A section of water that is usually deep and quiet; frequently found below rapids and falls.

Port/Starboard. Secret code for right and left; terms used by sailors to confuse landlubbers. These terms are not used in canoeing.

Rapids. Portion of a river where there is appreciable turbulence usually accompanied by obstacles. *See* **Falls.**

Riffles. Slight turbulence with or without a few rocks tossed in; usually Class I on the International Scale of River Difficulty.

River left. Left side of river when facing downstream.

River right. Right side of river when facing downstream.

Rock garden. Rapids that have many exposed or partially submerged rocks necessitating intricate maneuvering or an occasional carry over shallow places.

Roller. Also **Curler** or **Backroller;** a wave that falls back on itself.

Scout. To look at a rapids from the shore to decide whether or not to run it or to facilitate selection of a suitable route through the rapids.

Section. A portion of river located between two points. *See* **Stretch.**

Shuttle. Movement of at least two vehicles to the take-out and one back to the put-in. Used to avoid having to paddle back upstream at the end of a run.

Slide rapids. An elongated ledge that descends or slopes gently rather than abruptly and is usually covered with only shallow water.

Souse hole. A wave at the bottom of a ledge that curls back on itself. Water enters the trough of the wave from the upstream and downstream sides with reversal (upstream) current present downstream of the trough.

Spray skirt. A hemmed piece of waterproof material resembling a short skirt, having an elastic hem fitting around the boater's waist and an elastic hem fitting around the cockpit rim of a decked boat.

Standing wave. A regular wave downstream of submerged rocks that does not move in relation to the riverbed (as opposed to a moving one, such as an ocean wave).

Stern. The back end of a boat.

Stopper. Any very heavy wave or turbulence that quickly impedes the downriver progress of a rapidly paddled boat.

Stretch. A portion of river located between two points. *See* **Section.**

Surfing. The technique of sitting on the upstream face of a wave or traveling back and forth across the wave when ferrying.

Surfing wave. A very wide wave that is fairly steep. A good paddler can slide into it and either stay balanced on its upstream face or travel back and forth across it much in the same manner a surfer does in the ocean.

Technical white water. White water where the route is often less than obvious and where maneuvering in the rapids is frequently required.

Thwart. Cross pieces used to reinforce the gunwales of an open canoe.

Trim. The balance of a boat in the water. Paddlers and duffel should be positioned so the waterline is even from bow to stern and the boat does not list to either side.

Tuber. A person who chooses to travel downstream with his or her rear end protruding through the center of an inner tube. No matter which side s/he paddles on, s/he goes in circles. IQ equivalent to the vegetable part of the same name.

Undercut rock. A potentially dangerous situation where a large boulder has been eroded or undercut by water flow and could trap a paddler accidentally swept under it.

Upstream ferry. Similar to **Downstream ferry** except the paddler faces upstream. *See also* **Surfing.**

Index

Index of Maps